D0559564

TALES FROM THE PITTSBURGH STEELERS SIDELINE

TALES FROM THE PITTSBURGH STEELERS SIDELINE

A COLLECTION OF THE GREATEST STEELER STORIES EVER TOLD

DALE GRDNIC

Sports Publishing books may be purchased in bulk at special discounts for sales promotion, corporate gifts, fund-raising, or educational purposes. Special editions can also be created to specifications. For details, contact the Special Sales Department, Sports Publishing, 307 West 36th Street, 11th Floor, New York, NY 10018 or sportspubbooks@skyhorsepublishing.com.

Sports Publishing® is a registered trademark of Skyhorse Publishing, Inc.®, a Delaware corporation.

Visit our website at www.sportspubbooks.com.

10 9 8 7 6 5 4 3 2

Library of Congress Cataloging-in-Publication Data is available on file.

ISBN: 978-1-61321-089-5

Printed in the United States of America

The Pittsburgh Steelers have an extremely devoted fan base, so I'm dedicating my second book to my biggest group of fans: My parents, Steve and Catherine Grdnic, passed away early in my career. My dad's brothers, Mike and Frank Jr., who are deceased as well. Uncle Frank urged me for years to write another book. It's a shame he wasn't around to see it completed. My father-in-law, Ken Scharding, also passed away after my first book. He and his wife, Barb, were key components in one of its chapters. Finally, I would be remiss if I didn't include my wife, Denise, who suggested I make the dedication to the aforementioned group. Denise and I reached our 11th anniversary while I was in the midst of writing this book, so I wasn't able to spend a lot of time to celebrate. That was fine with Denise, because she has always been so proud of me. And I couldn't have accomplished anything without her.

Contents

Acknowledgments

There are many who deserve credit for assisting me in bringing this project to fruition, and Niels Aaboe, my editor from Skyhorse Publishing, is at the top. His guidance and sharp eye were a tremendous help throughout the entire process. Once I got started, many interviews needed to be arranged. Lynne Molyneaux, the Marketing and Community Relations Manager for the Steelers, was instrumental in securing contact information. Lynne works with the club's alumni, and if she didn't have a telephone number on file she tracked it down. Her support and assistance were crucial to my success. Brothers Dan and Art Rooney Jr. were also a big help. Lengthy interviews with them provided a tremendous amount of background information, as well as memorable stories to last a lifetime. Many current and former players were also helpful. If any of them tire of talking about their NFL careers, they didn't show it. That was appreciated. So, thanks to Andy Russell, Frank Atkinson, John Binotto Sr., Bill Priatko, Mike Wagner, L.C. Greenwood, Rocky Bleier, Walter Abercrombie, Tim Worley, Roy Jefferson, Gary Dunn, John Banaszak, Robin Cole, J.T. Thomas, Larry Brown, and Jeremy Staat. Players like you provided many reasons for the Steelers Nation to cheer over the years and information for guys like me to write a book.

Introduction

Most Steelers fans probably know that former No. 1 draft picks Ben Roethlisberger, Troy Polamalu, Maurkice Pouncey, David DeCastro, Plaxico Burress, Lawrence Timmons, Ziggy Hood, Cameron Heyward and even 2013 first-rounder, Jarvis Jones, are expected to play crucial roles for the club this season.

But do you know the name of the Steelers' initial No. 1 pick? You've probably heard the name before, but not related to football. However, when the franchise made William Shakespeare its first-round selection in the initial NFL Draft in 1936, the running back from Notre Dame was among the top college football players in the nation.

Like many Steelers from those early years, Shakespeare never made it in the NFL. Those who did and remained with the Steelers, who were called the Pittsburgh Pirates from their inception in 1933 through 1939—just like the city's Major League baseball team—basically toiled in anonymity because the team was so bad.

But it was those players who paved the way for future Steelers, the ones who took owner Art Rooney Sr.'s dream and made it a reality. Rooney Sr. certainly had a starring role in that regard. The "Chief" kept the team afloat throughout World War II, mergers with the Philadelphia Eagles in 1943 and Chicago Cardinals in 1944, and into the 1960s despite on-field struggles.

This collection of stories attempts to meld those early decades, when the Steelers were the league's lovable losers, with teams from the 1970s—which were among the most successful in the NFL's history—and more recent years when Hall-of-Famers needed to be replaced and future teams were built.

Subjects for these stories were chosen by a panel of one—me—and the chapters run chronologically, because that was the easiest way to do it. Some of the people that I interviewed made extensive contributions to the franchise—past, present, and future—while others were basically footnotes, but interesting nonetheless.

There was wideout Roy Jefferson, the team's MVP one season and trade bait the next, and running back Walter Abercrombie, who had the unenviable task of trying to replace the legendary Franco Harris. Then, there's Tim Worley, not the first and likely not the last player who had a promising career derailed by extensive partying. Fortunately for Worley, he turned his life around and helps others through motivational speaking for Worley Global Enterprises.

Then, there was the story of John Binotto Sr. His career with the Steelers is more of a note, as he was a seldom-used fullback from Duquesne in 1942. But Binotto Sr. is among the premier members of a dwindling group. Born in 1919, Binotto Sr. will be 94 on November 24, 2013, and is among a handful of oldest living former Steelers players.

There are other tales about more famous Steelers, and this is by no means a comprehensive list. However, I'm hopeful that this work can shed some light on things that Steelers fans never knew about their favorite NFL franchise and more importantly, bring a smile to the face of everyone who reads it.

Chapter 1

The 1930s

The Inimitable Chief

"Never allow anyone to mistake kindness for weakness," was a popular quote by Arthur J. Rooney Sr., the Chief. That's why this kind, generous man was strong enough to lead the Pittsburgh Steelers—and the entire NFL, for that matter—from their darkest days into prosperity.

Long before the Steelers and the NFL became the billion-dollar business that they are today, there was Arthur J. Rooney Sr., who later was known as the Chief. He was an AAU welterweight boxing champion and as tough as any NFL player. He was invited to the 1920 Olympics but had to decline the offer. The Chief also was deeply religious and helped many with his generosity throughout his nearly 90 years on Earth. He paid the $2,500 entrance fee for an NFL franchise in 1933 and named it the Pittsburgh Pirates. This also was the name for the city's professional baseball team, and the Chief loved baseball. So, he named his new football franchise after his favorite baseball team.

The Chief had many passions back then, such as his family, fine cigars, football, baseball, boxing, and betting on horses at the race track. It's been said that the Chief paid the franchise fee with winnings from a big score at the track. That entrance fee, which actually would be about $45,000 today, was substantial for anyone during those Depression-era days. And it probably did come from track earnings, but it wasn't from the huge score, as many believed.

Just ask Art Rooney Jr., the Chief's second son. Art Jr. was the Steelers director of scouting and player-personnel matters during the 1970s and much of the '80s. He is currently the team's vice president.

"Dad and I were going to see a movie about the Saratoga (N.Y.) race track, and I was a teenager, I think," Art Jr. noted. (The 1945 movie was *Saratoga Trunk*, with Gary Cooper and Ingrid Bergman. So, he actually was 10.)

"This got him reminiscing, and he really opened up to me," Art Jr. added. "That wasn't a very common occurrence, and he got to talking about going to the race track. I knew all the stories, even at that age, so I asked him about his big day. He told me it was more than $300,000, and it happened several years after he already owned the team."

The event reportedly occurred in 1936, with the amount listed at about $336,000. That's actually more than $5.5 million by today's standards when converted for inflation. Those winnings, as well as many other successful days at the track, helped the Chief keep the team afloat during those early years when money was tight and just covering expenses was often difficult.

"You know," Art Jr. said, "Pittsburgh was a huge college football town back then, and the NFL wasn't high on the public's radar. College football was king, and Pitt [the University of Pittsburgh] had a national-championship team."

The Pitt Panthers claimed five national titles before the Chief debuted an NFL franchise in Pittsburgh—1915-16, 1918, 1929, and 1931—and they also were national champs in 1934, '36 and '37. Art Jr. also noted that Carnegie Tech (now Carnegie Mellon University) had some success, with a 19-0 victory in 1926 against Knute Rockne and national power Notre Dame on its resume, while city school Duquesne and Washington and Jefferson College consistently sported solid programs as well.

The new NFL team also had to contend with the Pirates pro baseball team for a portion of its season. It played in the first World Series and won the event in 1909 and 1925 before losing to a powerhouse New York Yankees squad in 1927. Boxing also was popular in Pittsburgh, as light heavyweight champion Billy Conn was a Pittsburgh native who battled Joe Louis for the heavyweight title in 1941 at the Polo Grounds in New York. Several other champions from lower weight classes also came from the area. So, it wasn't easy for the Chief to maintain his team's popularity, let alone its roster and payroll.

"In the early 1930s, the guys only played 2-3 years," Dan Rooney said. "The '40s, it was different because of the war, but in the 1930s it was tough to get a good team together because the players changed all the time."

Dan, the Chief's eldest son, is the team's chairman and runs it with his son, team president Art Rooney II. Dan noted that the club did not win many games during the 1930s for several reasons. The Pittsburgh football Pirates played for seven seasons during that decade. They were 3-6-2 in 1933, 2-10 in 1934 and 4-8 in 1935 before a top mark of 6-6 in 1936. The Pirates fell to 4-7, 2-9 and 1-9-1, respectively, from 1937-39. So, it clearly was a struggle.

"Dad was a phenomenal businessman, and he knew how to handle the payroll and pay the bills, even if he had to cover expenses out of his pocket," Art Jr. said. "But he could do it, because he was doing very well betting on horses. He could keep expenses down, but a lot of times he had to pay out of pocket."

The NFL's Pirates also had five head coaches during the 1930s. Forrest "Jap" Douds led the way during their debut season, and Luby DiMelio took over in 1934. Joe Bach was the head coach during the 1935 and '36 seasons, but Johnny "Blood" McNally—a halfback from St. John's University in Minnesota—ran the team from 1937-39. McNally also played for the Pirates in 1934 and from 1937-39. Walt Kiesling replaced McNally during the 1939 season.

"Dad liked all those guys," Art Jr. said. "They were his friends, but players and coaches came and went all the time during the '30s. It was difficult to keep anybody in those years, and it was really tough to field a good team with the roster changing so often. But Dad did the best he could."

Despite an ever-changing team, from coaches to players, the Chief probably remembered nearly all their names. It was a talent that some possess, but few mastered it like the Chief, Art Jr. said. He really had a knack for remembering names, and he spent time getting to know as many players as possible.

"I found out later that he worked at it," Art Jr. said. "Sometimes, he wouldn't go to the opening days in training camp when all the rookies were there. He preferred to wait for a while after the roster thinned out.

"He told me that he couldn't remember all their names, but he wanted to remember them. He liked to talk to them when they came off the field. He asked each one about his hometown to try to make him feel at ease."

That's why the Chief was revered by the Steelers players, much like Dan Rooney is today. Outside linebacker Andy Russell, who was a Steelers rookie in 1963 and also played for the team from 1966-76, said that the Chief made an immediate impression on him as a fresh-faced rookie.

"He was at every practice, walking around the field to check things out, and it didn't matter if it was raining or snowing," Russell said. "The Chief was always there. So, owning the Steelers wasn't just a hobby for him. He treated us all like a family. He really cared. The Chief was a special man, well-loved by everyone.

"He came into the locker room after every practice and game, patted each guy on the back. He asked us how we were doing and took an interest in each one of us. So, it was a family atmosphere. You could go in and talk to the Chief and Dan if you had a problem or any issues, and that meant a lot to the players. It was then, and it still is a terrific organization. And the Chief started it all."

Art Jr. told several other stories to help define his father. Those tales centered on the Chief's generosity and gregarious personality. The Steelers take charter flights nowadays to their road destinations, so there's no need to file through an airport. But that wasn't the case in the early years, when the majority of travel was done by train. And no matter where he went, the beloved Chief was recognizable, especially in the Pittsburgh area.

"He couldn't go through an airport or train station or anywhere, really, without being stopped," Art Jr. said. "And he would talk with everybody. Many times, he almost missed the flight. That's just the type of guy he was."

There was at least one occasion when the Chief's fame did not precede him. It seems that one day, the Chief decided that the ashtrays in the lobby at the Steelers offices needed to be cleaned. So, dressed casually in a golf shirt and trousers, the Chief went on a mission to empty all the ashtrays. A rookie player approached him and talked with him for a few minutes.

"I guess the kid told him he was doing a good job," Art Jr. said. "Joe Greene came along and asked the kid what he was doing. He told Joe that he was talking to the janitor. Joe said: 'That wasn't some janitor you spoke to. That guy owns the team and signs your checks.'

"Joe probably said a few other things, too, but we probably can't print them. That kid was shaking after being chastised by Joe Greene, but the Chief didn't let anything like that bother him. He never talked down to anyone. I believe that's why he was so well-loved by everyone."

And he remained that way until his death in 1988. As the end neared, the Chief lay in a bed at Mercy Hospital in Pittsburgh, with his family by his side. A nurse approached Dan and Art Jr. to say that an older gentleman told her he was a very good, personal friend of the Chief. Art Jr. continues the story.

"He told Dan and me that he was Jimmy from the airport, and he knew all of us," Art Jr. said. "Apparently, this man carried our luggage at the airport, and he did that for more than 20 years. This qualified Jimmy, in his mind, to be the Chief's personal friend. We really didn't remember him, but he knew us."

And nearly everyone referred to Art Rooney Sr. as the Chief, but no one called him that to his face. There was nothing derogatory about it, but it just wasn't done. It didn't matter who did the talking, they didn't call Art Rooney Sr. the Chief. And nobody referred to him as the Chief when he was within earshot.

Art Jr. noted that his younger twin brothers, Pat and John, were responsible for the moniker. The twins liked "The Adventures of Superman," the television show based on comic book characters, that ran from 1952-58 on ABC.

"The guy who ran the newspaper where Clark Kent and Lois Lane worked was called Chief, and the twins liked that,"

Art Jr. said. "So, they kind of hung that nickname on our dad. A couple players and media guys picked it up after that."

The television character, Perry White, was the Editor-in-Chief of the Metropolis-based *Daily Planet* newspaper. Cub reporter-photographer Jimmy Olsen always called his boss "Chief," but Mr. White didn't appreciate the nickname.

"The guys in the media, they probably were the only people who called my dad Chief," Art Jr. said. "I had a secretary back in the day, and I had her about a year. My dad was in the room with a bunch of people, including her and some other secretaries, and she responded to something my dad said.

"She said, 'Thanks, Chief.' My dad didn't say a word, but all of those other secretaries stared her down. They couldn't believe she called him Chief to his face. They burned a hole right through her with those stares. I don't know why nobody would call him that, but I guess they didn't know how he'd react."

The Chief probably wouldn't have cared.

A Man Called Blood

Despite being pushed into athletics by his father during high school, John Victor McNally Jr. could not compete with his peers. The reason was quite simple. He was much younger and not as physically mature. McNally graduated high school at age 14 and started to fill out when he got to Saint John's University in Collegeville, Minnesota, where he eventually lettered in football, baseball, basketball, and track. He transferred to Notre Dame after three years to play for Irish head coach Knute Rockne but eventually was dismissed from the team when the coach of the freshman squad wanted to make him a defensive tackle and McNally balked at the move. He believed he should stay on offense, and he later was proven to be correct.

In 1924, before college graduation, McNally and a friend rode his motorcycle to Minneapolis to try out for the semi-pro football team there. But since the two still had college eligibility remaining, they needed to come up with fake names. Along the way, they saw a theater that showed the movie *Blood and Sand* with Rudolph Valentino. McNally's life and surname would change from that point. McNally told his friend to be Sand, while he would be Blood. And the colorful legend of Johnny Blood began. By the time he got to Pittsburgh's second-year pro football team in 1934, Blood was well-traveled, to say the least. And his off-field antics matched his on-field accomplishments.

"My father took a chance on Johnny, first as a player, then as a coach," Dan Rooney said in his autobiography. "Though he would find his way into the Hall of Fame, during his time in Pittsburgh, his performance on the playing field paled in comparison to his performance off the field."

Johnny Blood played for the Milwaukee Badgers in 1925-26, the Duluth (Minnesota) Eskimos from 1926-27, and he spent the next season with the Pottsville (Pennsylvania) Maroons, their last in the NFL. In 1929, Blood joined the Green Bay Packers and was among the best receivers in the league when they won three straight championships from 1929 through 1931, which was his best season. Blood was 6-foot-1 and 188 pounds with a combination of power and speed that helped him lead the NFL with 78 points on 13 touchdowns. He had 10 receiving touchdowns, a record for a running back, ran for two more scores and also returned one of his six interceptions for a touchdown.

Blood arguably could be given credit for the first Lambeau Leap, as the mercurial superstar reportedly climbed a fire escape, slid along an eighth-story ledge and leaped about six feet into the air to get through Packers coach Curly Lambeau's open window to persuade his boss to give him an advance on his salary. Blood also was known to have run atop a moving train on occasion, but only because a much larger teammate was chasing him. But that's another story to be told another day. Lambeau gave Blood the money, he survived the escapade, the Packers won another title, and everybody involved was happy.

"They pay me to score touchdowns," Blood once said during an interview with the media about his off-field antics. "The swagger, I give 'em for free. [But] I didn't spend my whole career on fire escapes. I had fun. I broke a few rules, but I got the job done on game day."

Blood stayed in Green Bay through the 1933 season until he was traded to the Pirates. He returned to the Packers for the 1935-36 seasons and won another championship before leaving there to be the Pirates' player-coach from 1937-39. His final season was with the Buffalo Tigers in the AFL in 1941.

The Chief, who claimed losses of $10,000 during the 1934 season with Blood as a player, made him a player-coach in 1937. Blood would go AWOL for a game and was winless in nine consecutive games, including the first three of 1939, so the Chief replaced him with Walt Kiesling. Blood finished with a 6-19 record, while Kiesling coached from 1939-40, 1941-44 and 1954-56. He was 30-55-5 overall. Kiesling was a co-coach with Greasy Neale in 1943 with the Steagles, the combined Steelers and Eagles, and a co-coach with Phil Handler in 1944 with the Card-Pitt team, the combined Chicago Cardinals and Pittsburgh. These mergers helped the team stay viable during the World War II years.

Green Bay Packers and Pro Football Hall-of-Fame wide receiver Don Hutson had a solid career at Alabama from 1932-34, and he got his first look at Blood shortly after that. Hutson was interviewed after induction into the Packers Hall of Fame, and Blood was among the topics of discussion.

"I played in the college all-star game and then went to, I believe, Stevens Point [Wisconsin] the next day where the Packers were going to play an exhibition game," Hutson said. "We came out on the field, and the Stevens Point Marines, or whatever they were, came out on the field. [And] all of our team went over to say hello to a guy on the Stevens Point Marines.

"It was Johnny Blood. I never heard of him. He had quit the team or [Coach Curly] Lambeau had run him off or something the year before. I don't remember what, and here he was playing . . . he came back to play with the Stevens Point Marines against the Packers. The Packers didn't know he was going to be there at all.

"Well, when the game was over and the bus left to go to Green Bay, among our passengers was Mr. McNally," Hutson added. "He had made up with Lambeau, and he had joined back up with the team. So, he went back with us to Green Bay. That was my first look at him."

John "Blood" McNally was voted into the Pro Football Hall of Fame in 1963. He would not earn his college degree until 1946 after retiring from the game.

A Comedy of Errors

The title of an early work by William Shakespeare appropriately describes the way the Pirates played throughout the

1930s. But it's also apropos because the Bard's namesake was the team's No. 1 pick when the NFL held its first player draft in 1936 at Philadelphia's Ritz-Carlton.

The Pirates had the third overall pick and determined that William Valentine Shakespeare, a running back from Notre Dame, was just the guy to help them win. Johnny Blood couldn't do it as a player in 1934 or later as a player-coach, and it turned out that Shakespeare was "Much Ado About Nothing" as well. He never played for the Pirates or any other NFL team for that matter. In fact, only two of the team's nine picks during that initial draft—fifth-round pick Wayne Sandefur, a fullback from Purdue; and eighth-round pick Ed Karpowich, a tackle from Catholic University—actually played for the Pirates. However, neither made much of an impact during his brief time with the club.

Shakespeare the football player always claimed to be a descendent of the Shakespeare from the late 1500s and early 1600s, but appeared to be headed to a career on the gridiron after a successful stint as a triple-threat player at Notre Dame. As a senior with the Fighting Irish in 1935, Shakespeare completed 19 of 66 passes for 267 yards. He also ran for 374 yards and four touchdowns and averaged 40 yards per punt to lead Notre Dame in all three categories. However, his top accomplishment that season was tossing a game-winning touchdown pass with 32 seconds remaining in an 18-13 Irish victory against Ohio State. It was the initial meeting between Notre Dame and the Buckeyes and was voted by the Associated Press as the best game during the first century of college football. This Shakespeare clearly had some game, as far as football was concerned.

Shakespeare finished third in the initial Heisman Trophy voting behind winner Jay Berwanger from Chicago and Army's

Charles R. "Monk" Meyer. Berwanger didn't play in the NFL, either. Shakespeare started to work for the Cincinnati Rubber Company that year and remained with the company until his death in 1974. He spent the final 15 years as the company president. Early in his tenure with the rubber company, Shakespeare entered the U.S. Army and commanded a machine-gun platoon in 1943. As a captain, he served in Germany and Northern France. During his military career, Shakespeare was awarded four battle stars, the Combat Infantryman Badge and the Bronze Star for gallantry during the Battle of the Bulge. More than two decades after his death, he finally was named to the College Football Hall of Fame. So, "All's Well That Ends Well," as far as Shakespeare's college football career was concerned. But his "Winter's Tale" in Pittsburgh turned out to barely be a footnote.

And Justice For All

By all indications, Byron "Whizzer" White was the first "bonus baby" in the NFL. When the Steelers selected him with the fourth overall pick in the first round during the 1938 NFL Draft, owner Art Rooney Sr. offered to pay the running back from Colorado the unheard of salary of $15,800 that first season. Sure, White was multi-talented and second in the 1937 Heisman Trophy voting to Yale quarterback Clinton Frank, but this would set quite a precedent for the league. And Rooney's peers weren't too happy about it.

"[It was] three times the going rate for the top players in the league," Dan Rooney said in his autobiography. "The other owners were furious. [Washington Redskins' owner] George

Preston Marshall accosted Dad, saying: 'What are you trying to do, ruin the league?' But as I said, Dad was desperate. His losing team was not only losing fans, it was losing money. He thought the Whizzer could turn the team around.

"[While] his new star impressed fans and opponents, even he couldn't overcome the erratic coaching and general poor play of the [Pirates]. To make matters worse, the Whizzer only played one season, then went on to Oxford as a Rhodes Scholar, then law school and eventually to a seat on the U.S. Supreme Court. Byron White was a gentleman, a scholar, and one of the greatest athletes I've ever seen."

Before White turned into a college All-American, editors at the university's newspaper believed he needed a nickname to get him noticed. They came up with Whizzer White. While the moniker basically rolls off the tongue—much easier than Byron—the player apparently never liked it. He reportedly disliked it because some might associate the nickname with a slang for urination. Unfortunately for White, he was the Whizzer the rest of his life, even though his accomplishments on and off the football field were noteworthy enough.

White's college career at Colorado finished with a flurry. As a senior, he guided the undefeated Buffaloes into the Cotton Bowl on New Year's Day in Dallas in front of an estimated crowd of 37,000. Despite a 28-14 loss to Rice, White shined brightly with Colorado's only scores, a touchdown pass and 47-yard interception return for a touchdown to give the Buffs a 14-0 lead. He ended the 1937 season as Colorado's leading rusher, passer, and kicker in the Buffaloes' single-wing offense and also played in the secondary on defense. White led the nation in rushing with a record-breaking 1,121 yards and tallied 122 points in just eight games. These records held until the NCAA added regular-season games. Despite all his accomplishments on and off the field, White finished second in the Heisman Trophy balloting following his senior football season.

White turned his attention to Colorado basketball during the winter and helped the Buffaloes go 10-2 in conference games. They competed in the debut of the National Invitation Tournament (NIT) at Madison Square Garden in New York City where they lost in the championship game. White also was supposed to play baseball in the spring but turned his thoughts elsewhere. He also was an academic All-American and received a Rhodes Scholarship to attend Oxford University in England. Few would turn down this marvelous opportunity.

Another chance already had presented itself, however, as the Pirates made White a first-round draft pick, and the Chief wanted to make him the highest-paid player in the NFL in hopes of increasing his team's win total and popularity. A meeting with the legendary Johnny Blood helped White agree to play football, and he delayed admittance to Oxford. The Pirates reportedly drew some 33,000 in attendance for his initial game at Forbes Field against the Giants.

Despite some individual success, White wasn't readily accepted by his teammates, as Art Rooney Jr. explained through an old story.

"The story goes that Whizzer White tried to run the ball in one game, and he didn't get anywhere," Art Jr. said. "The second time, the same thing happened. The next time they called his number, White asked his offensive linemen if they could open a hole big enough for him to get through it.

"The linemen supposedly responded: 'We make $4,000, and you make $16,000. Make your own hole.' With the way some of the other guys played, Whizzer probably had to make a lot of yardage on his own anyway, but he was a really good player and the first big-money player in the NFL."

Johnny "Blood" McNally was the Pirates head coach in 1938 and guided the Pirates to a 2-9 record, even though the Whizzer led the NFL in rushing that season and was an All-Pro selection. White served as Blood's presenter for his Pro Football Hall of Fame speech, and his former coach had this to say in a 1972 *New York Times* story.

"As a football player, [White] was a slashing runner who won the ground-gaining [rushing] championship with very little help from the rest of us," Blood said. "We were a bad team, winning only two games, and that is deeply significant. He did it alone."

White did not play football in 1939 and spent that time at Oxford. He also enrolled at Yale Law School but decided to return to the NFL to help defray the costs. White played for the Detroit Lions from 1940-41, led the league in rushing once again in 1940 and also was voted to the All-Pro team after both of those seasons. He likely would have been selected to the Pro Football Hall of Fame, had he played in the NFL a few more seasons, but destiny clearly took him in a different direction.

Following his football career, White served in World War II as an officer in U.S. Naval Intelligence with much of his time spent in the South Pacific. He earned a bronze star during that stint and developed a friendship with John F. Kennedy, who was then a naval officer. He returned to Yale after the war and graduated with high honors in 1946. White spent some time as a corporate lawyer, but in 1960 he turned his sights to politics and helped JFK win Colorado on his way to the presidency. White later served as the deputy attorney general under Kennedy.

On March 30, 1962, Kennedy appointed White to the U.S. Supreme Court as an associate justice. At age 44, he was the youngest nominee to serve on the highest court in the land. White served for 31 years and retired in 1993. He was nearly

85 when he died in 2002. Shortly after White's death, former Colorado athletic director Dick Tharp fondly recalled his initial meeting with the future justice, who was just a young lawyer in the late 1970s.

"As a young university lawyer, who had actually filed several briefs and petitions in the court addressed to Justice White in his 10th circuit role, I was overwhelmed by his kindness, forthrightness, and absolute unabashed interest in the athletic fortunes of the University of Colorado," Tharp said.

"[It] struck me, just as a fan at the time, about how informed he was [despite] dealing with a difficult workload and pending legal issues of the day. Whenever I saw him subsequently, he never failed to ask about the university and offer me personal encouragement. He always had an unmistakable presence about him.

"I had the wonderful opportunity to present and induct him as the first member of the University of Colorado Athletic Hall of Fame," Tharp added. "He represented the epitome of the reason we have athletic programs at a major university. . . . We will miss his presence."

White was inducted into the Colorado state sports hall of fame in 1965 and the University's athletic hall of fame in 1998. His football jersey No. 24 was the first to be retired by the Buffaloes. White made Colorado's all-century team in 1989 as the leading vote-getter, and he was a member of the NFL's team of the decade in the 1940s even though he only played from 1940-41.

There have been many talented players in the NFL over the years, and there have been some highly intelligent players as well. But few combined both attributes to the extent of Byron Raymond "Whizzer" White.

CHAPTER 2

The 1940s

NEW NAME, BETTER RECORD

Art Rooney Sr. changed his team's name to the Pittsburgh Steelers in 1940 to better represent the city's heritage. After going 22-55-3 during its opening decade (1933-39), the Chief hoped to change the franchise's fortunes as well. There was marked improvement in the team's record, 40-64 from 1940-49 with four winning seasons, but only one ended with a post-season appearance.

Walt Kiesling, who replaced Johnny "Blood" McNally as the Pirates head coach during the 1939 season, remained the club's leader under its new name. One thing remained the same that year. The Steelers selected running back Kay Eakin from Arkansas in the first round but promptly traded him to the New York Giants for offensive tackle Owen Lloyd "Ox" Parry, who would never play for the Steelers after three seasons with the Giants.

The club's first winning season came in 1942, as Kiesling guided the Steelers to a 7-4 record with rookie sensation

"Bullet" Bill Dudley leading the league in rushing. Dudley was a spectacular player for the Steelers, but success turned to sadness for Steelers fans when he joined the Armed Forces—along with many other NFL players—as the United States became involved with World War II.

"A lot of players lost two, three, four years in the war, and the Steelers lost their best player, Bill Dudley," Dan Rooney said. "That 1942 team, if there wasn't a war, that team would really have developed to be a pretty good team. But all the teams got taken apart. That's why we had to join the Eagles and have the Steagles [in 1943]."

Due to the wartime shortage of players, the Steelers combined with the Philadelphia Eagles in 1943, hence the name Steagles, and they hooked up with the Chicago Cardinals the next season. That team ingeniously was called Card-Pitt. The Steagles, who were 5-4-1 in their only season, actually were called Phil-Pitt. But the more catchy name stuck. Card-Pitt stumbled to an 0-10 mark in 1944. Kiesling and Greasy Neale shared coaching duties in 1943, while Kiesling and Phil Handler were co-coaches the following season. The consortiums ended after one season each, and the Steelers returned in 1945. It took a while for the club to build a competitive team, but that's a relative term since the Steelers finished higher than third place only four times in the next 27 seasons and six total times from their inception in 1933 through the 1971 season.

The Steelers were 2-8 in 1945 and 5-5-1 in 1946, even with Dudley back from the war. Jim Leonard was the head coach in 1945, but the Chief went after Jock Sutherland to coach the squad in 1946. He stayed for two seasons. The Steelers improved to 8-4 in 1947, but that would be Sutherland's final season as well. He died unexpectedly the following spring. John Michelosen took over the next year and was the head coach from 1948-51. He was 20-26-2 during that time. Other than the Steelers' last three coaches—Chuck Noll, Bill Cowher, and Mike Tomlin—and Raymond "Buddy" Parker, Sutherland was the only one with a winning record at 13-10-1 with a playoff appearance in 1947. Under Sutherland's guidance from 1924 to 1938, the University of Pittsburgh was 111-20-12 with 79 shutouts and four undefeated seasons. The Panthers won national titles in 1929, 1931, 1934, 1936, and 1937, and they played in four Rose Bowls.

"Pitt had a national-championship team and was very popular," Art Rooney Jr. said. "So, Dad tried to bottle that by hiring the Panthers' former coach, Jock Sutherland, and it worked out pretty well in the short term. Jock already was a legend in Pittsburgh, so Dad thought he'd generate more interest in the team.

"Jock wrote everyone who had Pitt season tickets and asked them to purchase Steelers season tickets. He was responsible for an increase in season tickets by 2,000. It was a big move, and it paid off. But the Steelers needed some big-time players, because Jock traded Dudley in 1947. They didn't get along."

The Steelers were 8-4 in 1947, the most wins in franchise history until 1962, and qualified for the post-season with a second-place finish in the East. But they lost in the playoffs, 21-0, to the Philadelphia Eagles. The Steelers ended the decade with a 4-8 record in 1948 (tied for third place) and 6-5-1 mark in 1949 (second) but did not qualify for the playoffs after either season. The Cleveland Browns, who debuted in the All-American Football Conference (AAFC) in 1946, won the league championship all four seasons (1946-49). They utilized more of a pass-oriented offense under head coach Paul Brown and record-setting Hall-of-Fame quarterback Otto Graham.

The Steelers were somewhat hesitant to change to a passing offense or even a defense to stop it. NFL teams generally played a 6-2-2-1 alignment to stop the run, but when teams like the Browns took to the air, defenses were forced to change to the now-standard 4-3-4 scheme that the New York Giants developed to stop Cleveland's passing attack. The Browns maintained their early success rate after joining the NFL in 1950 and won the NFL championship that season. They also won the NFL title from 1954-55 and lost in the championship game three times from 1951-53. During the 10 seasons from 1946-55, with Brown as the head coach and Graham at quarterback, the Browns played in 10 league championships and won seven times.

In the NFL, the times were changing, and the Steelers had to adapt.

No. 1 Picks, We Hardly Knew You

The decade began with the continuation of an alarming trend for the Steelers, who rarely signed their draft picks if they didn't trade the choices away altogether. Thanks to their poor finish in 1939, the Steelers received the third overall selection in the first round during the 1940 NFL Draft and picked Kay Eakin, a quarterback from Arkansas. It's no surprise that Eakin never played for the Steelers, and neither did 1941 No. 1 pick, Chet Gladchuk Sr., an offensive lineman from Boston College. The only difference was that Gladchuk was selected in the second round. The Steelers traded their choice in the first round. Ironically, both ended up on the New York Giants roster during their respective seasons, and the two were teammates during the 1941 campaign.

They played sparingly for the Giants over the next few seasons, but the Steelers certainly could have used either of them instead of a crew of washed-up veterans. The Associated Press named Gladchuk as a first-team All-American with the Golden Eagles, so he was a solid pick by the Steelers. But Gladchuk never made it through training camp in 1941, and the Steelers finished 1-9-1 for three different head coaches. Bert Bell went 0-2, while Aldo Donelli was 0-5. Walt Kiesling returned for his second of three stints as the Steelers head coach and guided the club to a tie against the Philadelphia Eagles and win against the Brooklyn Dodgers before capping the season with consecutive losses to go 1-2-1.

Gladchuk was with the Giants for parts of seven seasons, but played just 28 total games over three years. He played seven games in 1941, all 11 in 1946, and 10 in 1947 before taking a year off. Gladchuk returned to professional football in 1949, but it was with the Montreal Alouettes of the Canadian Football League. He participated in all 12 games that season and helped that team win the Grey Cup for the first time as CFL champs.

Gladchuk was just 50 when he died in 1967, but it was easy to track down his son, Chet Gladchuk Jr. The younger Gladchuk was a football letterman at Boston College, but his athletic achievements actually can be measured off the field. For the past dozen years, Gladchuk has been the Director of Athletics at the U.S. Naval Academy, guiding the Midshipmen athletic programs to one of the most successful periods in the school's history.

There actually was more information available on Gladchuk Jr. than on his father. Even though he wanted to do more, the son couldn't add much, either.

"I would love to help, but I was only 16 when my dad passed away, and I really have no insights on the subject," Gladchuk Jr. said. "I was so far removed from it. My mother could have been a valuable source for you, but unfortunately she has passed as well."

The Year the Steelers Finally Got It Right

It was 1942, and World War II raged into its third year. The Steelers were coming off a pitiful 1-9-1 record (for the second time in three years) that earned them the No. 1 overall pick in the upcoming NFL Draft. They selected triple-threat running back William McGarvey "Bullet Bill" Dudley with the choice and quickly learned it was the correct decision. Dudley made an immediate impact with a 55-yard touchdown run on opening day and a kickoff return for another score in the second contest. He led the NFL in rushing in 1942 with 696 yards and five touchdowns on 162 carries (4.3 average), caught one pass for 24 yards, and also was 35-for-94 passing for 438 yards and two scores. Dudley excelled on special teams as well with 18 punts for a 32-yard average, 20 punt returns for 271 yards (14.0), and 11 kickoff returns for 298 yards (27.0) and two touchdowns.

Those cruel football gods, who had not held the Steelers in high esteem throughout the team's previous nine years in existence, as well as Axis powers Germany, Italy, and Japan, worked against them once again. The Steelers did not make the playoffs, but their 7-4 record in 1942 was a franchise best. And there finally was hope for the future for Art Rooney Sr.'s venture into the NFL. However, after the Japanese attacked Pearl Harbor on December 7, 1941, the United States was all in for World War II and began drafting all eligible young men to fight for their country. NFL rosters were tapped to increase military forces for the Allies, and Dudley enlisted in the U.S. Naval Air Corps. Since he had not yet turned 21, he needed parental consent and didn't get it. By the time he enlisted in the U.S. Army Air Corps in September, still before his rookie year, there was an influx of recruits. So, he couldn't begin training for three months and was able to play that first season for the Steelers.

The United States was rocked by World War II, and the NFL was no different. Many of its members, including the Steelers, had to fight for survival. In order to keep his franchise in Pittsburgh, the Chief had to merge with the Philadelphia Eagles in 1943 and the Chicago Cardinals in 1944. Dudley missed both those seasons, as well as much of the 1945 campaign. Before Dudley could fly any missions for the U.S. Army Air Corps, he had to attend basic training in Florida and a flight school in Texas. In the interim, he joined Army's football team and led the Black Knights to a 12-0 record. Dudley was named the most valuable player. After the war, he played in three more games for Army against all-star teams.

Dudley returned to the Steelers for the final four games during the 1945 season and picked up right where he left off. In a game against the Chicago Cardinals, he ran for two touchdowns and kicked two extra points to become the Steelers' leading scorer that season. He also rushed for 204 yards, and returned three kickoffs for 65 additional yards. Dudley returned to the Steelers in 1946 and was just as spectacular with a team-best 604 rushing yards, 10 interceptions returned for 242 yards, and 27 punt returns for 287 yards. He became the only NFL player to lead the league in four unique statistical categories and earned the league's MVP award for his performance, but the club also got a new coach in Pitt legend Jock Sutherland. That was the beginning of the end for Dudley.

"Bill Dudley was still a good player, even though he lost a few key years to the war," Dan Rooney said. "But he and Jock didn't get along, so he was traded to the Detroit Lions. He finished out his NFL career with the Washington Redskins."

Dudley lasted until 1953 after three seasons with Detroit (1947-49) and three with the Skins (1951-53). He didn't play a lot in the running game during his first two seasons with the Lions, but Dudley caught 47 passes in that time for 13 total touchdowns. In 1949, he ran for 402 yards and three scores and added 27 catches for two more. Dudley ran for 737 yards and three TDs during his first two seasons in Washington and also had one catch for a score in each season (1950-51). Dudley did not play in 1952 and while he got into all 12 games in 1953, he was used sparingly with five rushes for 15 yards. He did not score a touchdown, but his body of work prior to that lackluster finish still earned Dudley induction into the Pro Football Hall of Fame in 1966.

It was a fitting end for Dudley and the Steelers as well, because they let another superstar slip away.

The Last of a Dying Breed

There are no former Steelers players still alive from those teams in the 1930s, and just a handful are still around from the 1940s. John Binotto Sr. is among them. The 5-foot-10,

185-pound fullback came to the Steelers from Duquesne University in 1942. Binotto is believed to be among the oldest living former Steelers. He was born on November 24, 1919, and still lives in the Pittsburgh area.

"I went to Cecil (Pa.) High School, and I had to walk home nine miles every night after practice, because they didn't have a sports activities bus," Binotto said. "That's how dedicated I was. I don't know if there are any other former Steelers who are my age and still living.

"There might be a couple of them, but I don't drink and don't really go to any functions that the Steelers put on. I know that all my Duquesne people are gone. We had a great Duquesne team. We were undefeated, untied, and uninvited to a bowl game (in 1941)."

With head coach Buff Donelli leading the way for that 1941 team, the Dukes finished the regular season as one of three undefeated, untied teams, led the nation in scoring defense, rushing defense, and total defense. The 1941 Duquesne defense surrendered just 21 points all season. Only one other team—Mississippi, with 21 points allowed in 1959—has given up 21 or fewer points in a season since. In 1941, Donelli had the distinction of coaching two teams at the same time, as he also guided the Pittsburgh Steelers. He eventually had to choose between the two and decided to stay at Duquesne. But Binotto moved on from that Dukes group to the Steelers.

"I got connected with the Steelers through Art Rooney, but I didn't hear from Art after he first called me," Binotto said. "And when Joey Walsh, an agent for the Cleveland Rams came around, he asked me if I was signed up with the Steelers. I told him I didn't hear from Art, and I saw he already hired a fullback.

"So, when Walsh asked me to sign with the Cleveland Rams, I said that was OK. So, I ended up with the Cleveland Rams, but when Art found out he sent two of my old Duquesne teammates—Petchel and Platukis—and they traded me for them so I could go back to the Steelers. And I went back to them."

John Petchel (1942-1945) and George Platukis (1938-1942) both played for the Rams in 1942 and had decent NFL careers. The fullback the Steelers signed was Joe Hoague from Philadelphia. He had 65 carries for 168 yards and one touchdown with the Steelers. He also had two punts for a 44-yard average and one interception. Born in Massachusetts, Hoague played for the Steelers from 1941-42 and also played for Boston in 1946. Thanks to the trade, the 22-year-old Binotto was back with the Steelers, his second NFL team in 1942. He tallied 57 yards on 16 carries (3.6 average) in just seven games as a part-time fullback. Binotto primarily was a blocker for rookie sensation Bullet Bill Dudley and also played special teams. He had two punt returns for 25 yards.

"Since I wasn't playing much, I asked Art what I could do because he already had a fullback, and it probably wouldn't get any better for me," Binotto said. "I had heard from the Philadelphia Eagles that they needed a fullback. Art told me that if I wanted to go down there, he would take care of me.

"So, he sent me to Philadelphia. He really was like my agent. He took care of me when I was in college and eventually brought me to the Steelers. Since I basically was an extra on offense, a blocker, and played on special teams, I wanted to play more. The Eagles wrote me a letter to see if I was interested, and I went down there for a couple games."

Binotto really didn't get an increase in playing time in Philadelphia and was credited with just one carry for minus-10 yards. Like many NFL players during that time, as well as other Americans, Binotto got a call from Uncle Sam to join the United States with the Allied Forces in World War II.

"After my rookie year in the NFL, I went into the U.S. Air Corps," Binotto said. "I flew the B-25s and B-17s. Then, I got out after three years. When I came home, I went to work for the Veterans Administration in Johnstown, Pennsylvania.

"They started up a semipro [football] league there and asked me if I wanted to play. I signed up right away and played for two years for the Johnstown Clippers. Then, I retired. My football career was over."

During World War II, Binotto flew the Boeing B-17 Flying Fortress and North American B-25 Mitchell bomber, but he never went overseas. He was sent to Columbus, Mississippi and flew for the Gulf Coast Command.

"I was glad that they didn't send me to London, because I had three brothers on the ground in Germany," Binotto said. "So, I told them that I don't want to get into a B-17 and shoot at my brothers. . . . I was very fortunate to not have to go to Europe, but I had enough to do over here.

"So, I put in my time in Columbus and then, I retired. My brother-in-law was a P-51 fighter pilot in Britain, against the Germans, and he paid me a visit in Mississippi. He told me he was getting out, and since the war was over I decided to get out, too. So, that was it."

For Binotto, the final football tally was one NFL season and nine games with three different teams—the Cleveland Rams, Pittsburgh Steelers, and Philadelphia Eagles—in 1942. His top accomplishment on the football field was playing with future Hall-of-Famer Dudley.

"He was my right halfback, and he was fast as hell," Binotto said. "I'd be up at the line, and he'd be on the right. I'd toss him the ball, and he'd run for a TD. He was quite a player, the best one the Steelers had back then.

"I was surprised when I read that he passed away a few years ago [February 4, 2010]. Well, at my age, I guess a lot of the old-timers are gone. Duquesne had that Sweet 16, but I'm the only one left. They're all dead, except me."

And that likely makes Binotto among the oldest living former Steelers players.

Nowhere to Go but Up

The Steagles finished 5-4-1 in 1943, but the Card-Pitt combo was a woeful 0-10 in 1944. The club drafted three notable players in 1943: No. 1 pick Bill Daley, a fullback from Minnesota, along with late-round selections Max Kielbasa and Nick Skorich. Kielbasa, a running back from Duquesne, played two games for the Steelers in 1946. Skorich, an offensive guard, kicked around the league for a while with 32 games logged for the Steelers from 1946-48.

Daley is notable as a No. 1 pick who never actually played for the Steelers, yet he is among the oldest men with ties to the team. Born September 16, 1919, Daley spent the 1946 season with the Brooklyn Dodgers and Miami Seahawks, 1947 with the Chicago Rockets, and 1948 with the New York Yankees. Kielbasa is notable for his name. An NFL team from Pittsburgh would appear to be best-suited to draft a man named after a type of cured Polish sausage, a staple of the city and its many ethic suburban towns. Skorich was more notable as an NFL coach. He was a long-time assistant for several clubs, but he also was the Philadelphia Eagles (1961-63) and Cleveland Browns (1971-74) head coach.

The 1944 NFL Draft yielded little help for the Steelers, as No. 1 pick (10th overall) Johnny Podesto, a running back from St. Mary's, Calif., didn't even make the roster. Paul Duhart, a running back from Florida, was the club's first-round selection (second overall pick) in 1945. Duhart played just that one season for the Steelers and had seven yards and one touchdown on 11 carries in two games. He also played eight games for the Green Bay Packers and three for the Boston Yanks. Duhart also is among the oldest former Steelers. He was born December 30, 1920, in Montreal, Canada. Former Army Heisman Trophy winner Doc Blanchard was the Steelers' No. 1 pick, third overall, in 1946. However, the bruising fullback, a collegiate superstar, never played a game in the NFL. The 1947 team was among the Steelers' best squads in the early years, as it finished 8-4 to qualify for the post-season. The Steelers lost that Eastern Divisional playoff, 21-0, to the Philadelphia Eagles.

Hub Bechtol, a defensive end from Texas, was the No. 1 pick in 1947. Bechtol never played for the Steelers, but he spent three seasons with the Baltimore Colts from 1947-49. In the late rounds, the Steelers picked up Miami, Ohio, running back Ara Parseghian and Cincinnati tight end Elbie Nickel. Parseghian never played for the Steelers, but he spent two seasons with the Cleveland Browns (1948-49) before an injury ended his playing career. He made his mark in athletics as a head coach, primarily at Notre Dame (1964-74), where he won two consensus national championships and several other major bowl games. Parseghian also has the distinction of being among the oldest living men with ties to the Steelers. He was born May 21, 1923. Nickel played for the Steelers from 1947-57 and tallied 329 career receptions for 5,131 yards and 37 touchdowns.

The three-time Pro Bowl selection, Nickel, a tight end, was chosen among the top 33 players on the Steelers all-time team.

Dan Edwards was the Steelers' first-round pick in 1948, but he never played for them. His NFL career spanned from 1948-54, and he played for five different teams. He also played for a couple different Canadian Football League squads. Single-wing tailback Johnny "Zero" Clement, known for preferring to wear the No. 0, was with the Chicago Cardinals in 1941 and then signed with the Steelers upon returning from World War II. He played for them from 1946-48 and ran for nearly 1,000 total yards. His best season was 1947 when he tallied 670 yards rushing and four touchdowns on 129 carries (5.2 average). Born October 31, 1919, Zero also is among the oldest living former Steelers players.

"Johnny Zero, he was a nice guy," Art Rooney Jr. said. "He would take us kids fishing on a boat. He was only with us for a few years, but we all liked him."

In 1949, the Steelers selected Clemson running back Bobby Gage in the first round with the sixth overall pick. He played for the Steelers from 1949-50. He ran for 334 total yards (3.9 average) with three touchdowns in each season. The Steelers also selected Tulsa quarterback Jim Finks in the 12th round that year, and he picked up the club's passing game considerably from 1949-55. Finks completed 661 of 1,382 passes (47.8 percent) for 8,622 yards and 55 touchdowns with 88 interceptions. But he stretched the field for the Steelers, which the franchise had not done with any regularity during its history.

Finks also ran for 294 career yards and 12 scores, but his biggest NFL impact was in administration. He was the general manager for the Minnesota Vikings from 1964-73 and took the same position, as well as the executive vice president job, with the Chicago Bears from 1974-82. He worked with the Chicago Cubs in major league baseball from 1983-84 and took over the woeful New Orleans Saints franchise from 1986-92. When NFL Commissioner Pete Rozelle retired in 1989, Finks nearly took his place as well. However, while the old guard owners voted him to the position, newer owners abstained, and he did not get the requisite number of votes. A second vote was taken, and he was tied with lawyer Paul Tagliabue. A compromise was reached during a third voting session, and Tagliabue was named the commissioner. Finks was offered another position, NFL President in Charge of Football Operations, but he didn't accept it.

There are several others who could vie for the title of oldest living former player with ties to the Steelers. Don Looney spent 1940 with the Philadelphia Eagles and 1941-42 with the Steelers. He was born September 2, 1917, and is the oldest known living former Steelers player. And Ben Agajanian played for the Eagles and Steelers in 1945 and seven other teams during a career that spanned from 1945-64. He was born August 28, 1919.

Chapter 3

The 1950s

After the War

The 1950s began with much promise for the Pittsburgh Steelers, as the NFL moved into another era following World War II. Popular University of Pittsburgh player and coach John Michelosen, who succeeded Jock Sutherland in 1948, remained the Steelers head coach into the next decade. Michelosen was 32 years and two months old when he was hired by the Steelers, and for the next fourteen years he held the distinction of being the the youngest head coach in NFL history. When the Los Angeles Rams hired Harland Svare in 1962, he was four months younger than Michelosen had been when he was hired. The Steelers coach was still the youngest to open a season until the Oakland Raiders selected Lane Kiffin to be their new head coach in 2007.

Michelosen guided the Steelers to a second straight six-win season. They went 6-6 in 1950 after going 4-8 and 6-5-1 during Michelosen's opening two seasons behind the bench. However, after going 8-4 and reaching the playoffs in Sutherland's final season in 1947 and dealing with his stunning death before the 1948 campaign, owner Art Rooney Sr. expected more from his Steelers. So, he made another change, and Joe Bach returned for his second stint as the head coach, having guided the Steelers during the 1935-36 seasons. As NFL teams altered their offenses, the Steelers finally were the last to abandon the single-wing for the T-formation in 1952. Health concerns forced Bach to resign following the 1954 campaign, and the Steelers' coaching carousel continued its recycling mode. Assistant Walt Kiesling replaced Bach to mark his third stint as the head coach. His coaching tenure now spanned three decades, including the 1939-40, 1941-44, and 1954-56 seasons.

"There were different parts of the 1950s that you could differentiate," Dan Rooney said. "The early '50s were really good, and that team was one of the better teams that we ever had. In fact, one of the problems the Steelers had in the early days was that they had a good nucleus, but they never had any backups. It was so hard to make the payroll, and things like that made it difficult for them to afford to sign any backups.

"So, when someone on the team got hurt, they were in trouble. But in the beginning of the '50s, they had Jim Finks at quarterback, and he was an excellent quarterback. You had Elbie Nickel, an outstanding receiver, and some good offensive linemen. And Ernie Stautner was just phenomenal. He was a tremendous defensive tackle, but he also played some on offense."

Despite Rooney's accolades, the Steelers remained mediocre throughout much of the 1950s, sporting a record at .500 or worse from 1950-57. Only 6-6 marks in 1950, '53, and '57 kept them from reaching complete futility. The Steelers were 4-7-1 in 1951 and 4-8 in 1955 to fall to the low-water marks.

Bach's record during his two seasons (1952-53) was 11-13, which actually improved his coaching record a bit to 21-27 overall. Kiesling's final three-year run (1954-56) wasn't any better at 14-22. How he got hired for three separate coaching tenures speaks volumes about the Steelers back then. Kiesling was 30-55-5 during nine seasons as the club's head coach, and he should not have been asked to return for the final three years.

"At the end of the '50s, when Bobby Layne and Buddy Parker came in, they really had a good team. Bobby Layne was a great quarterback, too, so we had two of the Steelers' best quarterbacks just in the '50s," Dan Rooney said.

"Of course, there was [Terry] Bradshaw, but those two guys in the '50s were really good, too. On the line, there were guys like George Hughes. We had a good center, too, so there were a lot of good guys on offense."

Buddy Parker took over the coaching reins in 1957 and finally brought stability to the position, but it came at a cost. Sure, Parker was 51-48-6 during his tenure (1957-64), as the Steelers were .500 in his debut and followed that with three winning seasons. But with Parker, the Steelers could not build team depth or stock talent for the future, because he refused to use rookies from the outset. Parker played many grizzled, washed-up veterans that were good for the short-term, but never had a chance to stay for more than a few years.

The NFL primarily was a running league during its initial decades, and the Steelers were among the last teams to use the single-wing formation. Coach Pop Warner has been credited with creating this offensive style, which has a wingback aligned tightly near an end. Basically, the ball is tossed to the back, as opposed to handing it off. The T-formation has three backs in a row behind the quarterback, with the fullback in the middle and a halfback on each side.

"We were one of the last teams to use the single-wing," Dan Rooney said. "We used that until, maybe, 1952, and then we changed to the T-formation. The single-wing primarily dealt with an unbalanced line, with wideouts in the slot, and the quarterback basically was in the shot-gun formation.

"But the quarterback rarely got the ball. It generally was snapped to the back, while the wing-T had a balanced line with the quarterback under center. We stayed with the wing-T for quite a while, too. There was a little bit of razzle-dazzle with lots of fakes and inside handoffs."

Teams like the Cleveland Browns and New York Giants changed the NFL on both sides of the line. The Browns passing game was too good for the standard 6-2-2-1 defense, which was designed to stop the run. The Giants changed to a 4-3 scheme to handle the Browns passing game.

"When the other team started to throw the ball, defenses had to back up and drop the ends off the line," Dan Rooney said. "That's why the 4-3-4 was a better defense. The Giants invented that for games against Cleveland. With a lot of people on the line, it's tough to drop back quickly enough. That's why the 4-3-4 worked a lot better."

The Steelers also needed to change their drafting ideas and when they did, so did their fortunes.

The Big Four from 1950

The Steelers hit the jackpot in the 1950 NFL Draft with four players who would be long-time starters for the franchise. They selected Michigan State running back Lynn Chandnois with their No. 1 pick, the eighth overall selection, who played for the Steelers from 1950-56. Ernie Stautner, a defensive tackle from Boston College, was their second-round pick. He dominated the line from 1950-63. Offensive lineman George Hughes from William and Mary was a starter from 1950-54, and Penn State running back Fran Rogel was the club's eighth-round pick that year. He played for the Steelers from 1950-57. These four players were crucial to any success that the club had during the 1950s.

Lynn Chandnois

In seven seasons with the Steelers, Chandnois ran for 1,934 yards (3.3 average) and 16 touchdowns. He also caught 162 passes for 2,012 yards and seven more scores. His best season was 1953. Chandnois tallied 470 yards rushing and three touchdowns, as well as 43 catches for 412 yards.

Ernie Stautner

Stautner wasn't the biggest defensive lineman at 6-foot-1 and 235 pounds, but he quickly became the cornerstone of the Steelers defense and one of the top D-linemen in the NFL by using quickness, tenacity, and brute force. Stautner was selected to nine Pro Bowls and missed just six games in a 14-year career.

Steelers outside linebacker Andy Russell played with Stautner in 1964 and the veteran defensive lineman, in his final season in the NFL, made an immediate impact.

"He truly was an inspiration to all of us," Russell said. "There was one time when he came into the huddle, and his thumb was broken back against his wrist. There was a tear near the break, and his bone was sticking out. He had a compound fracture of the thumb. He took his thumb in his hand and wrenched it down into his fist, and he didn't show it to anybody. All he said was 'what's the defense.' He played with it like that for the rest of our defensive series.

"After we stopped them and came off the field, I watched him to see what he would do. I was the only guy who saw that he had a compound fracture. I saw the bone, so I thought for sure he'd go right to the doctor and they'd take him to the hospital. I really thought he was in trouble and in danger of getting a bad infection. But all he said was 'Gimme some tape.' They tossed him some tape, and he started taping his hand."

Russell said that Stautner continued to tape his hand until it formed a huge club. Stautner returned to the game and never missed a down the rest of the way. Apparently, he made some pretty big plays as well.

"I couldn't believe it, but he pounded on the other team the rest of the game," Russell said. "After the game, we went back into the locker room, and he finally went to the doctor. 'Hey, doc,' Ernie said. 'I think I got a problem.' I think he's the toughest guy to ever play for the Steelers. I'm not saying he could win a fist-fight, because Joe Greene would have kicked his butt at any time.

"But just playing with a compound fracture in his thumb shows his courage and commitment, and that's why he was an inspiration to me. Joe Greene was a very inspirational guy as well, but he came along many years after Ernie. Joe was the player of the decade in the '70s, and I don't think there was any player that did more for his team that Joe Greene. He was awesome, but Ernie was really something, too. He was a great player and way ahead of his time."

Art Rooney Jr. remembered Stautner ripping through the Cleveland Browns' offensive line and terrorizing the quarterback and running backs until an injury forced him to come out of the game.

"He never wanted to come out of games and rarely did," Rooney Jr. said. "But he seemed to be hurt pretty badly and couldn't shake it off. So, at halftime, they decided to give him a shot of Novocain. Well, whatever they gave him, it wasn't Novocain. It turned out to be something like sodium pentothal."

Apparently, Stautner continued to fade in and out of consciousness, and the people in the locker room went into a panic. The trainers and doctors were unsure how to handle the situation, but one person eventually had an idea.

"A doctor hollered out to get a priest," Rooney Jr. said. "Well, 11 of them showed up. It was a Sunday, for Pete's sake. Weren't they all supposed to be in church? Finally, one of the priests took Ernie by the hand and asked him if he wanted to confess. Stautner looked up at him and said, 'Father, listen good, because I'm goin' fast. I only have time for the highlights.' That was Ernie."

The German-born Stautner was an All-Pro selection four times, the career leader in safeties with three and third overall in fumble recoveries with 23. He also played some at offensive guard when needed. On October 25, 1964, Stautner became the only player to have his number (70) formally retired by the Steelers. The Steelers equipment personnel haven't handed out all the numbers, unofficially retiring about a dozen, but Stautner was the only one to have his officially retired. He was inducted into the Pro Football Hall of Fame on September 13, 1969, the first year that he was eligible.

"I remember one time against the New York Giants, it was really a close game," Dan Rooney said. "And Ernie sacked their quarterback on three straight plays. That was something that really wasn't talked about back then, the sack, but he was able to do that. So, he was just a terrific player, and that's why they used him on the offensive line on occasion. He was just so strong.

"There were a lot of guys bigger than him, but I don't think anybody was stronger. His biggest things were his strength and his knowledge of the game. He was an extremely bright guy, and he really knew how to use leverage. And he was able to play both ways when we needed it, at offensive tackle or offensive guard, and he was a terrific guy. A great player and a great guy."

Linebacker Bill Priatko, who was a rookie with the Steelers in 1957 when Stautner's career was at its midpoint, noted that the powerhouse defensive lineman made an immediate impression.

"I've always called him a small Joe Greene," Priatko said. "Mean Joe probably was about 275 pounds, and Stautner was maybe 235. But both were able to control the line. They were strong, athletic, and really knew how to dominate from the middle of the line. That's why they're both in the Hall of Fame."

Rooney noted that since Stautner was symbolic of the Steelers style of play from then until now—tough, hard-nosed, physical, and aggressive—they wanted to honor him by retiring his jersey No. 70.

"I don't think you could do it with everybody, but we thought about doing something else," Dan Rooney said. "But we don't use some other numbers. There's going to be a time when you just won't have enough numbers, with 80-some players in camp. That makes it tough."

Along with Stautner's number, the Steelers don't use Terry Bradshaw's No. 12, Franco Harris's No. 32, Jerome Bettis's No. 36, Mel Blount's No. 47, Mike Webster's No. 52, Jack Lambert's No. 58, Jack Ham's No. 59, Joe Greene's No. 75 and, as of 2012, Hines Ward's No. 86. Hall-of-Fame wideouts

Lynn Swann (No. 88) and John Stallworth (No. 82) have not had their numbers held out.

"You have to keep some of them open, especially the higher numbers and lower numbers, but we're going to do something to honor all our guys, especially the Hall-of-Famers," Dan Rooney said. "We don't want to copy anybody. You know, Dallas and Washington have those rings, but we had another idea. Behind my father's statue at the stadium, we maybe would put up a wall.

"The Hall of Famers, you have to have some reason for separation. We would do something bolder. I don't know how, but we'd have an architect look at this. And it would be very nice. There's a lot of room there. You know, my father always said he never had a player he didn't like. He meant it, but that's a tough thing to say. The same as Will Rogers, who never met a man he didn't like."

Stautner's play certainly put him a cut above and made him a shoo-in for any honor bestowed on former Steelers players.

Fran Rogel

Rogel was born and raised in Pittsburgh, and he attended Penn State University. He was picked in the eighth round in 1950 by the Steelers, and he played for them from 1950-57. He ran for 3,271 yards (3.6 average) and 17 touchdowns and also caught 150 passes for 1,087 yards and two scores in 96 career games. Rogel also was an effective kickoff returner, but he mainly ran the ball.

Rogel ran the ball so often for the Steelers, reportedly nearly every first down when the club was on offense, that fans developed a saying for him.

"Fran ran the ball on the first play and got a lot of first downs," Dan Rooney said. "And they had this thing where they said: 'Hey diddle diddle, Rogel up the middle.' The writer who covered the team, Bob Drum, said that all the time. The story goes that my father told him that we were going to pass the ball.

"Well, we threw a pass for a touchdown, but it was called back for an offside play. Drum said that happened so they wouldn't have to listen to my father call plays all the time. I guess they didn't want him to be right, and Rogel was pretty successful running the ball. He wasn't real big or fast, but he was tough."

Bill Priatko, who played at Pitt and was signed by the Steelers in 1957, wasn't just Rogel's teammate but a lifelong friend. Rogel suffered from Parkinson's disease and passed away in June 2002, and Priatko believed the pounding he took and simultaneously dished out might have contributed to the illness.

"He took so many hits," Priatko said. "They said at Penn State that he never heard the whistle blow and never believed he was down. He wasn't that big, but he was a tough guy, physically and mentally. I've never known another guy like him. He really had a lot of heart and desire, and he was my good friend."

Rogel led the Nittany Lions in rushing from 1947-49. Then, he came to the Steelers and had 900 carries in eight seasons or 112.5 per year. That's a lot of carries for those days. Rogel earned a trip to the Pro Bowl in his final season with the Steelers. The team's late owner, Art Rooney Sr., so admired Rogel that he once named one of his thoroughbred race horses after him. And when Our Man Rogel won a race, Rooney Sr. sent the player a photo with the inscription: "I hope Our Man Rogel has a heart as big as our man, Fran Rogel."

For those who got to see Rogel play, the answer was quite clear.

Better Late Than Never

The Steelers picked Alabama fullback Clarence "Butch" Avinger with their first-round pick in 1951, the ninth overall selection, but the key pickup that year was St. Bonaventure athlete Jack Butler. Ironically, Butler never played scholastic football at his prep-seminary school in Niagara Falls, Ontario, but finally went out for football at St. Bonaventure because his roommates talked him into it. He eventually became a starting wide receiver as a senior.

One of the NFL's top all-time cornerbacks, Butler actually played in the secondary by accident. His former coach with the Steelers, John Michelosen, thrust him into a game when a cornerback was injured. Butler played with reckless abandon in the secondary for the Steelers from 1951-59, a time when 350 pass attempts by an NFL team through an entire season was a lot. Still, in Butler's 103-game career, most assuredly cut short by a severe knee injury during the seventh game in 1959, he tallied 62 takeaways: 52 interceptions and 10 fumble recoveries.

Butler continued to make an impact on the NFL after his playing career ended. For 45 years, he was the executive director of the BLESTO scouting combine, training scouts who would go on to become NFL general managers and team executives. Butler and Dick "Night Train" Lane were the only two cornerbacks selected to the NFL's 1950s Team of the Decade. Still,

Butler's amazing accomplishments on and off the field went largely unrecognized until 2012. That's 53 years after his career ended with the knee injury and 48 years after he initially became eligible, Butler was enshrined in the Pro Football Hall of Fame by the Seniors Committee. Fortunately, Butler, born November 12, 1927, was still among the living when elected. He passed away in May 2013, less than one year after he said the following after his presentation in Canton, Ohio.

"I never envisioned being here in Canton," Butler said after he was presented for induction by his son, John. "This induction is the highest honor I've achieved in my professional career. I am truly honored to be included with all these great players here.

"I have been very fortunate and have a lot to be thankful for. I was born with the talent to play football, had the motivation to become the best player I could be, and also was fortunate enough to play in the great city of champions—Pittsburgh."

Butler's interception total was second all-time when he was forced to retire due to the knee injury, which also was the first time he had to miss a game during his nine-year career that spanned 103 games to that point. His 52 career interceptions rank him 14th on the all-time list.

TALENT ABOUNDS
ED MODZELEWSKI

Maryland fullback Ed Modzelewski was the sixth overall pick by the Steelers in 1952. While his time in Pittsburgh was largely forgettable—just 195 yards rushing and three touchdowns, along with 11 catches for 109 yards—he later had solid seasons with the Cleveland Browns from 1955-59. Modzelewski had 292 carries for 1,050 yards and eight touchdowns from 1955-56 to go with 23 receptions and two more scores.

Ted Marchibroda

In 1953, the Steelers took hometown quarterback Ted Marchibroda from Franklin, Pennsylvania, with the fifth overall pick in the first round. After a successful college career at Detroit and St. Bonaventure universities, he elevated the team's passing game during the 1953 and 1955-56 seasons. Marchibroda also played for the Chicago Cardinals in 1957, but his best season was 1956 with the Steelers and was the only time he played all 12 games. He completed 124 of 275 passes (45.1 percent) for 1,585 yards and 12 touchdowns with 19 interceptions. They weren't Hall-of-Fame numbers, but Marchibroda made an impact on the NFL in another capacity.

After several seasons as the offensive coordinator for the Washington Redskins (1972-1974), Marchibroda became the head coach of the Baltimore Colts (1975-79). He also was the offensive coordinator for the Chicago Bears (1981), Detroit Lions (1982-83) and Philadelphia Eagles (1984-1985) before moving on to the Buffalo Bills. He was their quarterbacks coach from 1987-88 and offensive coordinator from 1989-91 before taking on two more head coaching positions. He returned to the Colts, only this time they were based in Indianapolis (1992-95), and ended his career with the Baltimore Ravens (1996-98) a couple years before they won their first Super Bowl.

John Henry Johnson

With their second-round pick in 1953, the Steelers selected bruising running back John Henry Johnson after a solid collegiate career at St. Mary's College in California and Arizona State University. Instead of signing with the Steelers, Johnson played in Canada for the Calgary Stampeders because he got a better contract offer from them. He lasted just one season in the CFL, but the best was always in Johnson's future. His most productive seasons came when he was in his early to mid-30s, and they were with the Steelers. But that time would have to wait, as Johnson had two other stops before joining Pittsburgh.

Johnson returned to the United States the next season and signed with the San Francisco 49ers. He is best remembered for being a member of the 49ers famed "Million Dollar Backfield." That fantastic foursome was composed of quarterback Y.A. Tittle, fullback Joe Perry, halfback Hugh McElhenny, and fullback Johnson. All four are enshrined in the Pro Football Hall of Fame. Perry was elected to the Hall in 1969, McElhenny in 1970, and Tittle in 1971, but Johnson would have to wait. The group was an offensive juggernaut during its first season together in 1954.

Tittle completed nearly 58 percent of his passes for 2,205 yards and nine touchdowns that season, easily his most yardage in 10 seasons in San Francisco. He also ran for 68 yards and four scores. Perry ran for 1,049 yards and eight touchdowns to become the first back in NFL history to surpass 1,000 rushing yards in consecutive seasons. He had 1,018 the previous year with 10 scores. They were the only two seasons that he reached the 1,000-yard plateau. He averaged 6.1 yards per carry in 1954. The elusive McElhenny never ran for more than the 916 yards he had in 1956, but he averaged eight yards per carry on his way to 515 yards and six touchdowns in six games in 1954. Johnson's best years were ahead of him, but he ran for 681 yards (5.3 average) and nine touchdowns during his first season in San Francisco. So, just those four players accounted for 2,313 rushing yards and 4,518 total yards.

After three seasons with the 49ers, Johnson was traded to Detroit and led the Lions to the 1957 NFL championship. He had 621 yards rushing and five touchdowns and added 20 catches for another 141 yards. Ironically, the Lions rallied from a 27-7 second-half deficit to beat the Niners, 31-27, for the Western Division title and then routed the Browns, 59-14, in the championship game. Johnson was powerful, fast, and elusive with excellent vision and balance. And at 6-2, 225 pounds, he could deliver hits as well as take them. Johnson was adept at using a stiff arm to shed tacklers and also didn't shy away from throwing a punishing block for his teammates. This combination made Johnson quite intimidating.

"You've got to scare your opponent," Johnson said during an NFL Films interview with Steve Sabol. "I can run away from a lot of guys after I get them afraid of a collision with me, [but] I always dish out more than I can take.

"[But] when you're a running back, a good running back, guys do a lot to try to intimidate you. They twist your arm and twist your leg. They bite you and rub their hands in your eyes. They do everything to intimidate you. So, you have to counterattack. [And] I hit them with my elbow."

Johnson's blocking prowess wasn't just as a backfield lead on plays. He was a wall in pass-protection, according to Bobby Layne. The Hall-of-Fame quarterback played with Johnson in both Detroit and Pittsburgh.

"John Henry is my bodyguard," Layne told NFL.com after Johnson passed away. "Half the good runners will get a passer killed if you keep them around long enough, but a quarterback hits the jackpot when he gets a combination runner-blocker like Johnson."

It also didn't hurt that Johnson relished his role as a punisher.

"I like to hit, and I like to block. I like to block for the quarterback," Johnson told Sabol. "You have to protect the quarterback, so backs have to help do that. And I appreciate the opportunity to hit a guy and knock a guy down."

With the extremely potent offense in San Francisco, many believed the Niners were due to win an NFL championship, but problems on defense kept them from finishing ahead of first-place Detroit and second-place Chicago in 1954. "The Million Dollar Backfield" never accomplished more than it did in that first season and was disbanded in 1957 without winning a title when Johnson was traded to the Lions. He played in Detroit for three seasons and finally returned to Pittsburgh in 1960.

Two seasons later, at age 33, he rushed for 1,141 yards to become the first Steelers running back to surpass the 1,000-yard mark. He accomplished the feat again the next season with 1,048 yards. On one night in Cleveland, about six weeks short of his 35th birthday, Johnson ran for 200 yards on 30 carries with touchdown runs for 33, 45, and 5 yards. That night, Johnson and fellow Steelers running backs Clarence Peaks and Dick Hoak tallied 319 rushing yards on 56 carries to key the 23-7 upset against the Browns, who went on to win the NFL championship that season.

"We found a play that worked [against the Browns], and we ran it," Johnson noted to Sabol. "[And] they couldn't stop it."

Johnson ended his 13-year professional career with the Houston Oilers in the AFL. He tallied 6,803 yards rushing with 48 touchdowns and 186 catches for 1,478 yards and seven more scores. He also threw two touchdown passes and played defensive back briefly early in his career. He had one interception. Johnson was elected to the Pro Bowl after the 1954, '62, '63, and '64 seasons.

In 1987, after eight years as a finalist, Johnson was elected to the Pro Football Hall of Fame. About a year before he passed away, Steelers owner Art Rooney Sr. presented Johnson during his induction ceremony in Canton, Ohio. Johnson was grateful that the Chief gave him a chance and took time to be with him during this special time in his life.

"He got out of his sick bed and came over to Canton to make the presentation on my behalf," Johnson said. "I was confident someday that I would be here, but then on the other hand, I thought I might be dead since it had taken so long. Today, I feel that I finally have that respect, and I wanna tell you, it makes me feel damn good."

When he retired, Johnson was fourth on the NFL's rushing list behind Jim Brown, Jim Taylor, and former teammate Perry. He is fourth on the Steelers career list as well behind Franco Harris, Jerome Bettis, and Willie Parker.

Another Heisman, Another NFL Bust

The Steelers selected Notre Dame running back Johnny Lattner with the seventh overall pick in the first round during the 1954 NFL Draft. Lattner, who won the 1953 Heisman Trophy for the Fighting Irish and the Maxwell Award in 1952-53, played 12 games for the Steelers as a rookie. He ran for 237 yards and five touchdowns to go with 25 catches for 305 yards and two more scores, but that was it for his career. He joined the Air Force and suffered a severe knee injury during a game that prevented him from ever playing football again.

The Steelers also selected a Heisman Trophy winner in the mid-1940s who never played a down for them. Doc Blanchard, the 1945 Heisman winner for the United States Military Academy at West Point, was the third overall pick by the Steelers during the first round of the NFL Draft in 1946. Instead of playing pro football, Blanchard opted for a career in the Air Force and served from 1947-71 when he retired with the rank of Colonel.

The One That Got Away

With the sixth overall pick in the first round during the 1955 NFL Draft, the Steelers selected Notre Dame offensive tackle Frank Varrichione. Only the most ardent, and older, Steelers fan would remember Varrichione, even though he was a six-year stalwart on the club's O-line from 1955-60 and tacked on five more solid seasons with the Los Angeles Rams for an 11-year NFL career. Any player in any era would welcome that longevity, and few could argue that this was not a good first-round draft choice for the Steelers.

In the ninth round, however, the Steelers found a real gem. And they didn't have to look too far to find him. The only thing was, they didn't know what they had in Louisville quarterback Johnny Unitas. Steelers owner Art Rooney should have been familiar with Unitas, since he played high school football at St. Justin in Mount Washington, Pennsylvania. And his eldest son, Dan, played for competitor North Catholic. In fact, as seniors, Unitas was the first-team quarterback and Dan Rooney the second-teamer when the All-Pittsburgh Catholic League all-stars were named. Maybe that's why Unitas never made the Steelers. A more likely reason is that Walt Kiesling was the head coach for his third awful stint. He recorded a 30-55-5 overall record, a .361 winning percentage and just one winning record as the Steelers' head coach. That was Kiesling's 1942 club, just before the war decimated NFL rosters. And it's believed by many that the Steelers could have developed into a championship team if not for the war. But it happened, and the Steelers combined with the Eagles (Steagles) in 1943 and Chicago Cardinals (Card-Pitt) in 1944 with Kiesling as a co-coach. The Steagles were 5-4-1, but the next year Card-Pitt plummeted to 0-10. So, among the many low points for the Steelers with Kiesling calling the shots, the Unitas debacle has to be among the deepest.

"I passed for three or four touchdowns in a scrimmage, and I got away on a couple of 30-yard runs," Unitas told *Sports Illustrated* during a later interview. "But they never let me play in exhibitions."

Unitas moved on to the Baltimore Colts and tortured NFL defenses for 17 seasons. He finished a Hall-of-Fame career with the San Diego Chargers in 1973 and, in his final NFL season, threw for just 471 yards in five games. However, it made him the first NFL quarterback to surpass 40,000 career passing yards. Unitas threw 290 career touchdown passes, including at least one in an amazing 47 straight games. Despite the current pass-happy NFL, that remained a league record until 2012. United guided the Colts to the 1958 and 1959 NFL championships and 1970 Super Bowl title. They also played in the 1969 game, but Joe Namath led the New York Jets past the Colts for the championship trophy in Super Bowl III.

For the record, Jim Finks and Ted Marchibroda were the Steelers' top two quarterbacks in 1955. Finks started all 12 games and threw for 2,270 yards and 10 touchdowns with 26 interceptions. He passed for more than 189 yards per game. Marchibroda played in just seven games and was 24-for-43 for 280 yards and two touchdowns with three interceptions. The Steelers liked to run the ball that season as well and tallied nearly 1,300 yards on the ground. Fran Rogel was the top rusher with 588 yards, while Lynn Chandnois added 353 and Ray Mathews had 187. Rogel also had 24 catches, while Chandnois had 27 and Mathews added 42 receptions for 762 yards and six touchdowns.

Marion Motley

The Steelers had another future Hall-of-Famer on their roster after picking up bruising fullback Marion Motley from the Cleveland Browns in 1955. Motley, due to his hit-and-be-hit running style, was physically beaten when he got to the Steelers and played in just seven games with eight yards rushing on two carries. He primarily was used as a blocker, as the trio of Fran Rogel (588 yards), Lynn Chandnois (353) and Ray Mathews (187) combined for 1,128 yards and eight touchdowns on the ground. The group also caught 93 passes for 1,369 yards and six touchdowns, all by Mathews, with Motley as an escort.

"We were running out of players," Art Rooney Jr. said. So, we signed him to see what was left. (Steelers Hall-of-Fame cornerback) Jack Butler told me Marion was well-liked on the team, but really was out of gas by the time he got here. He only lasted seven games. I remember one time when Marion made a crack about our team, saying that playing against the Steelers was like running downhill. Our players and the press felt they could nail him on that one.

"However, Marion was quick-witted. He talked his way out of it. He said that many of our games at Forbes Field were played while the Pirates pitcher's mound was still raised, so he had a real advantage at those times because he was indeed running down a hill. We all laughed at that one."

Motley was among four of the first African-Americans to play professional football in 1946, one year before Jackie Robinson signed with the Brooklyn Dodgers. At 6-1, 232 pounds, Motley possessed imposing size to go with power, speed, and athleticism. In one game against the Steelers in 1950, Motley ran for 188 yards on just 11 carries, a spectacular 17.1 yards per rush. Motley had nearly 5,000 career rushing yards in nine seasons with an amazing 5.7 average yards per carry.

A Premium in Picks

The NFL faced some competition for college players when the All-America Football Conference joined the fray late in the 1940s and lasted four seasons. The AAFC was founded in 1944, began play in 1946, and closed shop in 1949. The NFL believed it needed to add a bonus pick from 1947 through 1958, and during that stretch each team received the No. 1 overall pick in the draft once to go with its usual first-round selection.

The Steelers chose Gary Glick, a defensive back from Colorado A&M, with their bonus choice in 1956. The club's first-round selection that year was Mississippi State running back Art Davis. Glick stayed with the Steelers from 1956-59, while Davis lasted only through the 1956 season and ran for six yards on five carries to go with one catch for nine yards. He didn't score a touchdown.

Glick played 34 games in four seasons with the Steelers, including 12 each as a starter in the secondary during the 1957-58 seasons. Glick played just two games for the Steelers in 1959 before being traded to the Washington Redskins. He played nine games for the Skins that year and 11 more in 1960. Glick played 11 games for the Baltimore Colts in 1961 and finished his career with the San Diego Chargers in 1963. He had 14 career interceptions.

Bill Priatko, a linebacker from Pitt, played for the Steelers just one season. But his still-keen memory from 1957 included some thoughts on Glick and the group that played for the Steelers in the secondary.

"Glick was a good defensive back, but I thought all those guys were pretty good back then," Priatko said. "There was this one guy, kind of a funny guy, whose name was Freddy Bruney. He was from Ohio State [1956-57], and he was a funny guy, a little bit of a character. There was Dick Alban from Northwestern [1956-59], Dean Derby from Washington [1957-61], Glick, and Jack Butler in the secondary. Those guys got most of the snaps.

"So, there were some good football players on that team, but we lost a lot of close games. A field goal here, a big play there, they made the difference that season when we finished with a 6-6 record. So, we only played 12 games in the regular season. And we played six preseason games. We got paid $50 a game for each preseason game. That was separate from our salaries, so that $300 in the preseason was big money."

The Steelers also had some amazing depth at quarterback that season. They selected Len Dawson from Purdue with the fifth overall pick in the first round during the 1957 NFL Draft, and they also signed Jack Kemp from Occidental College and picked up Michigan State's Earl Morrall after he spent one season with the San Francisco 49ers. Since he was a second-year player, Morrall was brought in to be the starter, and he did that for 11 games. Dawson got the other start and played in three games, while Kemp saw action in four games. Dawson lasted three seasons with the Steelers, while Morrall played two. And Kemp moved on after just one.

"We had three really good quarterbacks, and all three eventually moved on from the Steelers to have great NFL careers," Priatko said. "Buddy Parker was brought in to be the head coach that season, and he had that reputation of moving guys in and out. He really didn't care for rookies, either.

"And I don't think he worried about it too much, because it probably was foremost in his mind that he was going to bring in his buddy, Bobby Layne, from Detroit the following year. So, I think that's probably what prompted all of that. He was bringing in Layne to be the starter in 1958."

Parker coached Layne previously in Detroit, and the quarterback already was a legend. He helped the Lions win NFL championships in 1952, 1953, and 1957, and owner Art Rooney Sr. craved that level of success for Pittsburgh. Layne finished his Hall-of-Fame career with five solid seasons for the Steelers (1958-62), and the club was 33-28-3 during that stretch with just one losing season. But there were no championships. The Steelers were 9-5 in 1962 to place second in the East.

However, they lost the playoff bowl matchup for third place, ironically, to the Detroit Lions, 17-10.

"There were a lot of good guys on the Steelers when I got there, good players and good guys, and a lot of them came after my one season," Priatko said. "But we just never could get over the hump for the Chief. We wanted to win so bad, but like I said it was just a couple plays here and there that really hurt us.

"I only played the one season in the NFL and had a shot with three teams, but I always said that my greatest benefit and form of compensation with the Steelers was to put on the black and gold and play for a wonderful man like Mr. Art Rooney Sr. He was just a wonderful man, a great human being.

"No matter who you were on the squad, the No. 1 pick or a free agent, a rookie or a 10-year veteran, he treated everybody the same," Priatko added. "He made each player feel like he was the most important guy on the team, and since I also was from Pittsburgh that meant a great deal to me."

There were only 12 teams in the NFL in 1957 with 35 players on each roster, which means there were some 420 players in the league, and Priatko was among them. That's a marked difference from the 85 players that each of the 32 current NFL teams takes to training camp, the final 53-man rosters, nine-player practice squads and big money that even the most marginal player can make. The rookie minimum for the 2013 season is $405,000.

"We all had offseason jobs," Priatko said. "I sold Wrigley's gum. I called on wholesalers and chain stores and buyers like Thrift Drug store, A&P Market, Kroger's, lots of different places. I signed for a $500 bonus, and I thought I was a millionaire. Paul Horning was the first-round draft choice and No. 1 pick overall by Green Bay that year, and he signed for $2,000.

He was the Heisman Trophy winner and the top player coming out of college.

"So, that's what the money was like back then. I came from Pitt, signed with Green Bay as a rookie and made the ball club. Ray Scott was the announcer for the Packers, and he knew me from my Pitt days. He came into the locker room and congratulated me for making the team. It was a Tuesday, and the final cut had to be made. We had to cut four guys to get from 39 to 35."

Priatko noted that the Packers practiced on Wednesdays and Thursdays during the week, but he never made it to the end of that opening week. Packers coach Lisle "Liz" Blackbourn (from 1955-57) came into the locker room after the first practice and held a meeting, where Priatko was informed that the team had secured Pro-Bowl pass-rusher Carlton Massey, who was on an Army National Guard tour, but he got an early out. So, instead of missing the upcoming season, he could play for the Packers. That mean Priatko was relegated to the taxi squad.

"I basically had to clear waivers first, before I could go to the taxi squad, and that's when Buddy Parker picked me up for the Steelers," Priatko said. "So, that's how I ended up with the Steelers, but I always say that I was a Green Bay Packers player for a week."

Along with fourth-year player Massey from Texas, who'd had brief success with the Browns, Priatko ticked off names of Packers stars whom he met that season. The group included center Jim Ringo, rookie Paul Horning, receivers Billy Howton and Gary Knafelc, starting quarterback Babe Parilli from Rochester, Pennsylvania, and Bart Starr, who actually was the No. 3 quarterback behind Parilli and Hornung, who was a running back, pass-catcher, quarterback, and place-kicker. Hornung, Starr, and Ringo ended up in the Pro Football Hall of Fame.

"That group formed the nucleus of the great Lombardi teams," Priatko said. "They weren't champions just yet, but the foundation was laid. Once I got to the Steelers, I was able to be teammates with my lifelong friend, Fran Rogel, and another one of my good Pitt teammates, Richie McCabe. They were the only two guys I knew at that time when I checked in with the Steelers.

"I got to know the other guys real well after that, but it helped to already have two good friends on the team when I got there. I had a chance to go to the Brownies for a couple years after that to play for Paul Brown, and that's where I met my good friend Dick LeBeau. . . . Dick and I are still dear friends. We actually were roommates during training camp when I got to Cleveland, so you can make a lot of good friends in this business.

"And I certainly have been blessed in that regard," Priatko added. "I've been lucky, and I've been fortunate. So, I'm grateful for that. I'm also going to be inducted into the Western Pennsylvania Sports Hall of Fame in May [2013], so all kinds of things have happened to me because I played football. I only kicked around for three years or so, but it was enjoyable."

Priatko was only given credit for playing two games for the Steelers in 1957, and LeBeau—a fifth-round draft pick by the Browns from national champion Ohio State—also was cut by the Browns during the 1959 season. But he eventually hooked on with the Detroit Lions and played 14 spectacular seasons at cornerback. When he retired as a player in 1972, LeBeau had 62 career interceptions. Priatko explained why he was with the Browns that year, along with LeBeau, but it wasn't on record.

"Each team had its own rules," Priatko said. "In Cleveland, if you weren't on the squad for six games, you weren't considered a full-time or full-year squad member. Other teams were different. You could play in two games and be considered for a full year. So, it was a different league back then and tougher to make a team."

Priatko added to his Hall-of-Fame list when he left the Packers for the Steelers, as the club's No. 1 pick that year was Len Dawson. The rookie quarterback was 6-for-17 for 96 yards and one touchdown with two interceptions in three mostly forgettable seasons with the Steelers.

"Lenny Dawson, he was just a little guy," Priatko said. "I couldn't believe it. He wasn't very big at all, just a skinny, little kid. [As a player, Dawson was listed at 6-0, 190 pounds]. I asked Fran Rogel who he was. I thought he was the ball boy, so I was surprised when Fran told me he was the Steelers' No. 1 draft choice and a quarterback. He was out of Purdue, but you could see that he was sharp. And you could see that he had talent.

"The same could be said for Jack Kemp. He was a real good player, too. Later on, those guys did pretty well, because they matured and developed. And their talent really came out. Earl was a good quarterback for the Steelers, too. All of them—Len Dawson, Earl Morrall, and Jack Kemp—went on to better careers after they left the Steelers. But, like I said earlier, the Steelers were counting on Bobby Layne coming on board in 1958."

While Priatko only knew two of his new teammates before arriving in Pittsburgh, camaraderie was quickly built. The Chief, and others in the organization, promoted a family atmosphere that the players embraced. Priatko explained.

"We had Mondays off after a game and didn't practice until Tuesday, but we had to go down to our team headquarters—which were at the Roosevelt Hotel in downtown Pittsburgh—to pick up our game check," Priatko said. "Can you imagine that? I really can't see today's players doing that, but maybe they would have done whatever they had to do, just like us.

"Anyway, we usually got together on Monday nights to relax a little bit. Fran and I didn't drink, but Ernie Stautner could drink enough for both of us and maybe a few others as well. So, every Monday, about a dozen guys or so would go down to the Polish Club in Braddock. It was kind of a ritual for us. We would just sit around and sling the bull and have a few drinks, except for Fran and me. We just drank ginger ale, but all of us had a real good time.

"The Chief really loved it that we spent all that time together," Priatko added. "You know, like a family. And I know it's still that way, because I go down there to watch practice with Dick LeBeau just about every week. They have a good group of guys, just like we had in 1957, because that's the type of player the Steelers try to bring in. It doesn't always work out that way, but they try to do it. They have a lot of good guys and a lot of good coaches on that team."

Knee injuries cut Priatko's playing career extremely short, but he likely wasn't the only one. Rehabbing an injury basically was the player's responsibility in those days, Priatko said, and the longer the process the less of a chance there was for a comeback.

"The NFL didn't have the injured reserve list like now," Priatko recalled. "You got hurt, the team either waived you or signed you up for the taxi squad. I practiced with the team. I was just glad to be getting a paycheck every week."

During his time with the Cleveland Browns, Priatko likely mixed it up on a daily basis during practice against veteran offensive guard Chuck Noll, who was in his final season as a player. About a decade later, Noll became the head coach for

Priatko's hometown Steelers and developed into one of the most successful coaches of all time.

"Isn't that ironic," Priatko said. "Who would have ever thought I would make lasting friendships with two of the NFL's greatest coaches in that Cleveland Browns training camp in 1959, Chuck Noll and Dick LeBeau? Like I've said before, I'm just grateful for the opportunities presented to me thanks to playing football and the wonderful friendships that I've forged."

Priatko, who was born in 1931, resides in North Huntingdon, Pennsylvania.

A Disturbing Trend

The decade of the 1950s ended as strongly as it began for the Steelers with some good players being brought in via trades and other signings, but when Buddy Parker was the head coach from 1957-64 the club basically abandoned the annual NFL Draft.

In 1958, the Steelers traded their first-round pick and settled on West Virginia running back Larry Krutko in the second round. Krutko played 25 games for the Steelers from 1958-60 and was most productive during 1959 with 226 rushing yards and four touchdowns. He also caught 13 passes for 100 yards.

The key acquisition was quarterback Bobby Layne, who moved into the starting lineup immediately in 1958 and remained through his final NFL season in 1962. Layne completed about 49 percent of his passes for 9,030 yards and 66 touchdowns with 81 interceptions.

In 1959, the Steelers dumped their top seven draft picks and took Purdue running back Tom Barnett in the eighth round. He played in all 24 games with the Steelers from 1959-60, but accomplished much more as a rookie. He ran for 238 yards and one touchdown and caught seven passes for 52 yards and another score. That production dropped to just six carries for 25 yards in 1960 with no catches and no touchdowns.

More importantly that year, the Steelers selected Pitt defensive back Dick Haley in the ninth round. He ended up beginning his NFL career with the Washington Redskins and played for them from 1959-60. He also spent the 1961 season with the Minnesota Vikings, but then he returned to the Steelers. Haley played for his hometown team from 1961-64. He tallied 14 interceptions during his seven-year career with 13 coming for the Steelers.

Haley's biggest impact on the NFL, and the Steelers in particular, was as an evaluator of talent. He was the Steelers player personnel director from 1971-90 and held the same role with the New York Jets from 1991-2002. Haley's impact on the Steelers nowadays is slightly more indirect. His son, Todd, is the Steelers' offensive coordinator.

Chapter 4

The 1960s

The More Things Change, The More They Stay the Same

Raymond "Buddy" Parker became the eleventh head coach of the Steelers in 1957, and he remained in that role through the 1964 season. Parker was a good coach, the club's most successful to this point with a 51-48-6 record and five non-losing campaigns through eight tumultuous seasons. But the Steelers continued to trade draft picks and stick with most grizzled veterans who accomplished little to that point. There were just a few outstanding players on those Parker teams.

Owner Art Rooney Sr., the Chief, assembled a motley group in 1962 with Parker leading the way. The Steelers went 9-5 that season, a high-water mark for the franchise during its first 30 years, to earn the second post-season spot in that stretch as well. The Steelers were to face the Detroit Lions in the Bert Bell Benefit Bowl, better known as the Playoff Bowl. But it basically was the runner-up bowl, because it was for third place in the NFL, and it was played after the championship. The Playoff Bowl was played all 10 years in the 1960s at the Orange Bowl in Miami after the New Year's Day college game in that stadium.

There's some irony to that game between the Steelers and Lions on January 6, 1963. With former Cleveland Browns quarterback Milt Plum in a starring role, the Lions already had a victory against the Steelers, 45-7, in the regular-season opener less than four months earlier. And three former Lions stars—head coach Parker, quarterback Bobby Layne, and running back John Henry Johnson—were key performers for the Steelers that season. Layne threw for nearly 1,700 yards, mostly to wideout Buddy Dial (almost 1,000 receiving yards), while Johnson set a club record that stood for another decade, with 1,124 rushing yards.

But that wasn't enough for the Steelers, as Plum was the difference once again. He had already notched several big wins against the Steelers as the quarterback for the Browns and threw three touchdown passes for the Lions in their opening-day victory, but this game was close in the second half. With the score tied 10-10, Plum connected with Dan Lewis for a 74-yard game-changer to get into scoring range, and fullback Ken Web plowed in from the 2 to secure a 17-10 Lions win.

This game was the Steelers' second foray into the postseason, but it also was significant for uniform innovation. They debuted their trademark black helmets with the Steelmark logo on just the right side with three colored diamond shapes called hypocycloids. It was created by U.S. Steel Corp. and belonged to the American Iron and Steel Institute (AISI). Instead of the word "Steel" next to the gold, red, and blue diamond shapes, the franchise put "Steelers" on the helmet. And one of the most recognizable NFL symbols was born.

Unfortunately for the Steelers, that was the most positive aspect of the Playoff Bowl game following the 1962 season.

Sure, the Steelers went 7-4-3 for Parker in 1963, but eight straight losing seasons followed until the franchise's fortunes changed dramatically in 1972. Parker and the Steelers were 5-9 in 1964, and he was replaced by Mike Nixon, who was the head coach for just one season. Nixon led the Steelers to a 2-12 mark in 1965. The Chief replaced Nixon with Bill Austin in 1966. Austin remained through the 1968 season and compiled an 11-28-3 record. The on-field futility remained for three more seasons, which can be attributed to poor drafting practices, horrendous personnel decisions, and just downright bad luck, which permeated the franchise's history and remained throughout the 1960s.

Parker took TCU running back Jack Spikes with the team's first-round pick in 1960, but he never made the roster. Fred "The Hammer" Williamson, a safety from Northwestern, was brought in that year as well, but he played just one season. (Williamson later became an AFL all-star and was an announcer on *Monday Night Football* for a short time after a successful playing career. He is still working today as a film actor.) The Steelers' second-, third- and fourth-round picks in 1960 were all traded after that. The same thing happened in 1961 with a slight variation. The club traded its No. 1 pick and took Notre Dame linebacker Myron Pottios in the second round. Pottios played for the Steelers from 1961-65, the Los Angeles Rams from 1966-70 and Washington Redskins from 1971-73.

The Steelers traded picks 3-6 in 1961 and then selected Penn State running back Dick Hoak in the seventh round. Hoak was an amazing player with nearly 4,000 yards rushing and 25 touchdowns, as well as 146 catches for nearly 1,500 yards and eight more scores in 10 NFL seasons from 1961-70. Hoak also was a Steelers assistant coach for the team's running backs from 1972-2006. The Steelers brought in another running back in

1961, Dick Haley, who played for them from 1961-64. Haley played for the Washington Redskins from 1959-60 and then moved on to the Minnesota Vikings and finally the Steelers in 1961. He played 49 games for the Steelers, but was used primarily as a punt and kick returner. Haley already had worked for the Steelers for 17 years when he took over the scouting and player-personnel duties in 1987. His son, Todd, is the current offensive coordinator for the Steelers after nearly a three-year stint as the head coach for the Kansas City Chiefs.

The Steelers selected Ohio State running back Bob Ferguson with the fifth overall pick in the first round during the 1962 NFL Draft, but traded picks 2-6. In 1963, the draft insanity continued. The Steelers had the 11th overall pick and traded it. They got rid of picks 2-7 as well, so eighth-round choice Frank Atkinson—a defensive lineman from Stanford—actually was the No. 1 pick.

No. 1 with a Bullet

Frank Atkinson, the Steelers' No. 1 pick by default in 1962 because they traded away choices 1-7, was a talented rookie defensive lineman. But like the other first-year players on the Steelers that year, he had little to no chance to play.

"The way you get to be the team's No. 1 pick when you're drafted in the eighth round is that you get drafted by a club that hates rookies," Atkinson said. "Steelers head coach Buddy Parker and guys in that regime trusted a drunken veteran rather than a guy from a college all-star squad. That's just the way he was, but how I got drafted by Pittsburgh I'll never know."

Actually, the Chief told Parker to draft a few college players that year and keep some rookies on the squad. That didn't mean Parker had to play them, but on occasion he had no choice, according to fellow rookie that year, Andy Russell. The Steelers took Russell, an outside linebacker from Missouri, in the 16th round. He played for the Steelers that season, was off from 1964-65 and returned to play from 1966-76. He was the Steelers' defensive captain during his final 10 seasons.

"That rookie season Parker actually told us that he hated rookies," Russell said. "He said that we lose games, we're not any good, and he wanted to get rid of most of us. But the Chief wanted him to keep a few of us, so he said he'd probably do that. But most of us wouldn't be there the next year. So, Frank and I were lucky enough to make it. And we both played a lot that season.

"Frank really was a class guy, and he was from Stanford, so he was a real smart guy, too. He viewed playing pro football like being a ski bum in Aspen for one year between undergrad and graduate school. He started a lot of games his rookie year and played really well as a rookie. After that he went back to Stanford, got his MBA, and went right to work in the venture capital business."

The Steelers' 10th-round pick that year, quarterback Bill Nelson from Southern Cal, also made the team and eventually was the club's starting quarterback. He played for the Steelers from 1963-67. But Atkinson and Russell started almost immediately, even though neither planned to stay in professional football. Along with Russell and Nelson, Atkinson said a couple other rookies made the team, including Roy Curry, a "jack of all trades," and defensive back Jim Bradshaw. Curry was a wide receiver by trade and caught one pass in his only season, while Bradshaw played in 62 games from 1963-67 and tallied

11 interceptions, primarily in a reserve role. He had no career starts.

"For a club that didn't like rookies, we had a handful of guys from our rookie class make the team," Atkinson said. "And how we all got there is pretty amazing. There were questionnaires mailed out to various college players by all the teams, which is kind of bush league compared to the way things are done today. They asked you to fill out your height and weight. Your time in the 40, things like that, but I really didn't get any interest from Pittsburgh.

"I thought Dallas would be the team that would draft me. The San Francisco 49ers and Los Angeles Rams also showed some interest, but I think they were just filling out their filing cabinets. I think they did their drafting in those days out of Street and Smith's. You know, the old Street and Smith's sports publication. But teams had scouts in each region, and the Steelers' scout out here (West Coast) was a guy named Fido Murphy. He was quite a character."

While Atkinson played in all 14 games for the Steelers as an NFL rookie, along with the 1964 season in Denver, he never aspired to play professional football. Atkinson wasn't certain that he would sign with a team if drafted, and his father believed to be fair he should send a Western Union telegram to Dallas to tell the Cowboys that there was no guarantee that he'd sign a contract. Atkinson added that he didn't really think about the draft until the night of the event.

"I got a call at my fraternity house from a guy named Will Walls," Atkinson said. "I guess he was the overall head of the scouting department. He congratulated me on just having drafted me, but he never said what club it was. Later that night, and a few beers later, I found out it was Pittsburgh. Back in those days, I was a college football romantic. When I got to

Pittsburgh, eight of the nine guys in my draft class wanted to play pro football.

"I was the only one who just wanted to play college football at Stanford. But after I got drafted, I took it as a challenge to see how good the game would get and how well I could compete. I think the NFL was in its infancy, compared to college. Pitt probably outdrew the Steelers. There was no big TV contract, but there were a lot of NFL stars like Jim Brown, Y.A. Tittle, and Johnny Unitas. So, there was a lot of talent and more on the way from college football."

Atkinson still wasn't certain how things would play out with the Steelers, but he signed his first pro contract and returned to California. He had a few months off before training camp, so he "jumped on one of those tramp steamers [a ship] and went to Saigon, Vietnam." Atkinson was on a tourist visa, but the area's spirit was dampening a bit because the U.S. military had just started engaging in Vietnam, as there were about 5,000 instructors there.

"I was sitting in a bar in a harbor in Saigon," Atkinson said. "It probably was March 1963. There were enough military personnel in the country, so they had the Stars and Stripes newspaper available [with] a story on [Steelers defensive tackle] Big Daddy Lipscomb dying of an overdose. Everyone in Pittsburgh, everyone connected with the Steelers, believed it was a murder.

"As I recall, his arm was littered with needle marks, but everyone knew that he was fearful of needles. He wouldn't take pain-killing shots or anything like that. So, he was the last guy who would die from an overdose after extensive drug use. That's why everybody believed there was foul play, but I didn't think much about that. All I could think of was that my stock just went up.

"They drafted me to maybe inherit Ernie Stautner's position at defensive right end, and Big Daddy was the right tackle," Atkinson added. "When I got to camp, they worked me at right end a little bit, and they had given the right tackle spot to Lou Cordileone. He and I fought over that spot, but eventually I got the start. So, Andy [Russell] and I both started for the Steelers on defense as rookies."

The left defensive end was George Tarasovic, who played for the Steelers from 1952-53 and 1956-63, so that was his last season with the club. With five rookies eventually making the final roster, it appeared that the Steelers were easing into a youth movement through the draft. Still, Atkinson was not impressed. He had an agreement with people in the business school at UCLA to attend its graduate program, which usually took two years to complete. Atkinson needed three if he was going to attend only in the offseason.

"I had a deal to do one semester that spring and a second semester the next spring," Atkinson said. "Then, I had to do one full year of two semesters to finish. So, it would take me three years to get an MBA, but I also could play two seasons for the Steelers. So, I went back for the second season, but I think I might have strained the relationship a little bit. I held out.

"The standard clause in a standard contract said that the club had an option in a one-year contract to renew it the second year at 85 percent of the first year. That sounds kind of usurious, doesn't it? I told them I wasn't coming back for just 85 percent. I wanted the whole thing. I was a starter. But I got cocky with them, and that was stupid, probably the dumbest thing I've ever done."

Atkinson continued to chuckle throughout this part of the story, that continued with him saying he told the Steelers that his second season would also be his last. The Steelers apparently looked for alternatives to Atkinson playing on the D-line, and selected Ben McGee from Jackson State. His contract situation, along with McGee's development, was the beginning of the end for Atkinson with the Steelers. He played three games with the Denver Broncos in 1964.

Atkinson eventually completed his MBA at UCLA and immediately began a successful business career that has spanned some five decades. Atkinson was a Stanford legacy, as his mother and father both attended. The family was in the construction business, so Atkinson traveled quite a bit in his youth.

"Andy Russell and I became friends pretty quick," Atkinson said. "He was well-traveled for a young guy, because his father took jobs around the world for Monsanto, and we had a lot of similar interests. . . . Eventually, he would do business trips in various parts of the world, and he would stop to see me wherever I was at the time. And he always took Steelers players with him.

"We started out in Beirut, but when we got there it turned out to be the beginning of a 15-year civil war. So, we moved to Dusseldorf and set up a German operation for the company. Then, we gave up on Beirut and moved the headquarters for our European operation to London. I probably stayed six years overseas, from 1974-80. Andy came over after the first Super Bowl."

Atkinson is a managing principal and senior advisor for the Perreault Birmingham Group LLC in Menlo, Calif. The firm assists small- and medium-sized technology businesses in funding their growth beyond their start-up years. His venture capital work has continued to connect him with Russell, who has maintained a home in Aspen where the two occasionally get together. Atkinson has a daughter who lives about 10 minutes from Russell's place, so that's another connection. And there will always be the Steelers.

"I got to know David DeCastro out here, before he graduated from Stanford, and of course I took more of an interest in him when I found out he was drafted No. 1 by the Steelers," Atkinson said. "I even had Andy introduce himself to David when he got to Pittsburgh.

"I also gave him my copy of Roy Blount's book, *About Three Bricks Shy of a Load*, so he could learn a little bit of history about the Steelers. David's a great guy and a whale of a player. He's going to be a 10-12-year starter and Pro Bowl guy for the Steelers. He's a can't-miss player. I'm sure of it."

It takes one No. 1 pick to know one.

An Odd Journey

This paraphrased title from one of Andy Russell's three Steelers books is a perfect description of his life. A self-described corporate brat, Russell was born in Detroit and lived there for eight years. Russell's father worked for Monsanto Corp., and every time he got promoted the family moved. They lived in Chicago for 2 1/2 years, New York for 4 1/2 years, and then on to St. Louis for his scholastic years at Ladue Horton Watkins High School.

"I was a high school All-American and had 28 scholarship offers," Russell said. "My dad told me I could visit 4-5 schools, but not all 28. So, I had to pick a few schools to visit, but I wasn't getting out of the state. Dan Devine was the head coach at the University of Missouri, and I'm really thankful that I did not leave. I enjoyed the entire experience, not just the football, but that was great, too.

"We had some really good teams, ranked in the top 10. That's why I think Dan was underrated as a head coach. His teams were among the best in the country in the 1960s. He had a great record, a no-nonsense guy. He didn't put up with any foolishness. I mean, if a guy yawned in practice, he'd cut him. He was a tough guy. He left there and went to Green Bay and took them to the playoffs.

"They didn't make it the year before, so he turned them around pretty quick," Russell added. "But he didn't have the charisma that Vince Lombardi had, so they criticized him every chance they got. He went to Notre Dame after that and took them to the national championship. So, he was a great coach, in my opinion, and I feel very fortunate to have had him as my college coach."

Like most high school players, Russell played on both sides of the ball, a running back on offense and safety on defense. He was about 6-foot-2 and 200 pounds. As a junior running back at Missouri, Russell led the Tigers in rushing with 412 yards (4.1 per carry) and two touchdowns. He added seven catches for 100 yards and appeared to be destined for a big senior season. A bright future as an NFL running back also was in order, but Devine had other ideas.

"My senior year, Dan told me I would just play linebacker because I was getting too tired in the fourth quarter," Russell said. "I was upset. I didn't want to be a linebacker. But, all of a sudden, I'm a linebacker 100 percent of the time, and I led the team in interceptions. But I never thought I was going to be a pro. In fact, I really believed I didn't have a chance."

Russell participated in Missouri's ROTC program and already had committed to go into the service. He noted that if someone went regular Army, he had to go for five years. Commitment to the reserves was for two years, and Russell figured he would do the whole five because his parents already were in Europe. He could go to Germany and get to see his family more often. Russell eventually got to Europe and actually has traveled the world, but with several detours through Pittsburgh, even though he didn't plan it that way.

"There were six NFL teams in the East and six in the West, but there was no Combine before the draft," Russell said. "The teams sent out a questionnaire to various college players, and I got 11 of them. The first question was: 'Are you interested in playing pro football?' I answered no on all of them and sent them all back without filling out the rest of the questionnaire.

"The only team that didn't send me a form was the Pittsburgh Steelers, and they drafted me in the 16th round in 1963. They called me, and I told them they made a mistake because I had the military commitment. They wanted to know when I had to show up. I later was told that I had to be there in January 1964. I graduated in June 1963, so I needed something to do that fall."

Russell signed a rookie contract with the Steelers and went against his father's wishes. He believed it would humiliate the family, because his son would make a living by playing a game. The Steelers intervened so Russell wouldn't have to go into the military, but he honored a two-year commitment after his rookie year in 1963. He was deployed to Germany as an Army lieutenant, and returned to play for the Steelers from 1966-76.

"The guy I was playing behind went down with a terrible injury in the opening game against the Eagles," Russell said. "He had a massive concussion and swallowed his tongue. It was just terrible. They had to chop his teeth out to save his life. So, I had to go in during the first quarter of the first game, and that was my big break. I started the rest of the year and was a rookie All-Pro.

"Of course, the Steelers said I couldn't go into the military, but that wasn't an option. I signed a contract, but they said they'd get me out of it. I turned them down. I wanted to go to Germany for two years. So, it wasn't anything planned for me to play pro football after college. It just wasn't on my mind at all. In fact, I actually promised my dad that I wouldn't do it. But I broke that promise."

Russell told his father that he would play that rookie season and then spend two years in Germany. After that first year in the NFL, Europe was a breeze for Russell. The Steelers didn't have a practice field and worked out at South Park.

"Actually, it wasn't a real football field," Russell said. "It was just a space next to the horse track there. The rookies had to pick up rocks off the field. This was quite a shock for me, coming from the University of Missouri, which had 10 beautiful fields. Going from there, where all the fields were in great shape, to the professional level, it was hard to believe. Our locker room was an old house.

"I think it was an old medical building, and we dressed in the basement. It was amazing. I was very surprised with this setup. Wc had brand-new locker rooms at Missouri. Then, all of a sudden, I was in the pros, and it was very different. We went in there one morning, and there was a snow drift all over our pads. It had come through the walls, so it really was an interesting experience."

When Russell returned from his commitment to the Army, he rejoined the Steelers. Buddy Parker was no longer the head coach. He had been replaced by Bill Austin, who coached the Steelers from 1966-68 and was 11-28-3 overall with a 2-11-1 record in 1968. This prompted another coaching change.

"The Steelers hired Chuck Noll, and he was supposed to make a drastic change in our team," Russell said. "Well, we promptly went 1-13 that season, but the best was yet to come for Chuck and the Steelers. That's for sure. Chuck told us that he had been watching a lot of film from our previous games, and he knew why we didn't win a lot of football games. Chuck basically said that we just weren't any good, so he was going to have to get rid of most of us. And he did.

"Back in the '60s, when we were so bad, we were in a position to draft quality players. But no matter who we picked, more times than not they didn't even make the team. Then, after Noll came, we built nearly the entire team from the draft. Only five of us made it from the first team meeting with Chuck in 1969 to the first Super Bowl season in 1974. So, we had an entirely new team."

Only Russell, center Ray Mansfield, running back Rocky Bleier, offensive guard Sam Davis, and punter Bobby Walden met Noll in 1969, before his first draft, and remained with him in 1974. Russell's business career had taken off by then as well. Since the NFL was not the big business that it is today and its players were not millionaires, Russell had to work on a career that he would cultivate during the offseason. And that blossomed right along with his NFL career.

"Frank Atkinson, the Steelers' No. 1 pick my rookie year, kept in contact with me after that first season," Russell said. "He had developed a huge venture capitalist business, but decided to shut down all his offices in the U.S. and move to Beirut, Lebanon, in 1974. He was going to work for a Saudi with wealthy parents who also went to Stanford with him. I couldn't believe it.

"And he wanted me to visit him during the next offseason, after he got settled there, but I didn't want to do it. I had been to Beirut when I was in the military, and I didn't care for it. I told him I didn't want to go, but he kept bugging me. Finally,

I said I would go if the Steelers win the Super Bowl. We didn't even make the playoffs until 1972, so winning the Super Bowl was a long shot."

After missing out on the big game from 1972-73, even though they qualified for the playoffs for two straight seasons for the first time in franchise history, the Steelers went the distance in 1974. They beat O.J. Simpson and the Buffalo Bills in the opening playoff game and then won the AFC championship game at Oakland to reach Super Bowl IX in New Orleans. The Steelers faced quarterback Fran Tarkenton and the Minnesota Vikings, and the Steelers won, 16-6.

"Frank called me at the Pro Bowl in Miami," Russell said. "He watched the game in Khartoum, Sudan, and reminded me of my promise. I told him I would go to Beirut if I could make it a business trip and brought two really smart business guys with me. Because of that trip, we went around the world eight years in a row, giving speeches in Tokyo, Hong Kong, Singapore, Bangkok, places like that.

"After that first year, we took Ray Mansfield with us every year. He was my best Steelers buddy and also a very good speaker. One year, we took Lynn Swann, because the Undersecretary of the Ministry of Oil for Kuwait went to USC like Swann. He wanted us to come back, but I told him no unless he did some business with us. He said that would be OK if we brought Lynn with us."

Russell noted that he tried to bring a Steelers teammate with him every year, and the lengthy list included Mel Blount, Mike Wagner, and Jack Ham, as well as Mansfield and Swann. Mansfield was the Steelers center from 1966-76 and set a team record with 182 consecutive games played. After their playing careers ended, Mansfield and Russell maintained their business relationship. However, they also went on "wilderness adventures" together that primarily consisted of camping and hiking. Mansfield also went on his own quite a bit. He had a heart attack and died while hiking through the Grand Canyon in 1996.

"That's a hike we did three times together," Russell said. "I was sort of the instigator for these trips. I wanted to see the world. We did a canoe trip. I think it was 167 hours non-stop or something like that. We did the Himalayas. We started doing fourteeners in Colorado [mountains more than 14,000 feet above sea level]. Ray didn't like those, probably because of his heart issues.

"But I fell in love with it and finished all 53 in Colorado. If you do them all, it's called the Grand Slam. Some guy just did that in 11 straight days, but it took me 23 years. So, he's a track star. There are no fifteeners in Colorado or any of the 48 states. There are some in Alaska. There are 600 thirteeners in Colorado. I won't do those, but it's quite a task to climb those mountains."

As Russell also noted in his first published work in 1998, *A Steeler Odyssey*, his business trips occasionally were a little rougher than the hiking excursions. During a business trip to Bangkok, Thailand, Russell, was joined by Steelers cornerback Mel Blount and some other friends. After a long night out, Russell found out that Blount had been drugged and was in pretty bad shape.

"It was a scary situation," Russell said. "It could have killed him. He doesn't drink, so we left him in a bar talking with some Thais. We figured he couldn't get into any trouble, since he was sober, but they apparently gave Mel some sort of knockout drops and dragged him back to his room and threw him in there. But what they didn't know was that I was his roommate, so I was there.

"They probably were going to rob him. They didn't count on me being in there, so they tossed him in the room and ran down the hall. I guess they wanted all his money, but they didn't count on seeing me in there. That wasn't the end of the trip. We went to India, Calcutta, the Black Hole. Then, we went to the Himalayas, and Mel was still bothered by the drugging. He was really struggling.

"We made him go on a 31-mile hike through the Himalayas, but Mel rallied," Russell added. "What an amazing guy. . . . And it all started with that first trip in 1975, the one after the Super Bowl when we went to see Frank Atkinson. But we found out that the Saudis and Arabs invited us over there all the time, and the Minister of Finance sent his jet over to pick us up in Pittsburgh."

The Steelers got a lot more attention after they won their first Super Bowl, but after winning a second straight the national media attending training camp turned into international media.

"After one morning practice, I noticed some Japanese businessmen there," Russell said. "I asked Ray to come with me to talk to them. Nobody else paid attention to them, even though there were about 10 of them there. We directed them to our meeting rooms at lunchtime. One guy was the editor of Touchdown magazine in Tokyo, while the other guys were businessmen.

"One of those was the president of Sony Corp. We told them we wanted to go to their country, and we would do whatever they wanted us to do if they would also do business with us. All we asked was that they pay our expenses, no fee. We were doing major real estate transactions. The thing about the NFL in those days was that you didn't make much money, so you had to have a real job."

By the time his NFL career got rolling in 1969, Russell said that he already was making more money with his business ventures than he was paid by the Steelers. So, it was a significant amount.

"When I came back from Germany, I went back to Missouri for my MBA and finished it in two years, going in the offseason," Russell said. "And I eventually started my own business. I was making pretty good money, compared to what I made playing football, and that's probably the last time that will happen.

"It's a little harder to do today. I was selling deals for Wall Street. I quickly learned that I couldn't just do that business in the offseason. I had to keep it alive during the season as well. I went to meetings before practice and after practice. It was 24-7 work, but I loved every minute of it. It was exhilarating."

And it was all part of Russell's amazing Steelers journey.

No Player Was Bigger Than the Team

It seems that Steelers coach Chuck Noll agreed with "Star Trek" actor Leonard Nimoy, who starred as Vulcan first officer Mr. Spock in the series and ensuing movies. Spock said: "Logic clearly dictates that the needs of the many outweigh the needs of the few or the one."

Few disputed that wide receiver Roy Jefferson, the club's second-round pick from Utah in 1965, was the Steelers' best player in 1969 when Noll was hired. Jefferson tallied 13 catches and one touchdown as an NFL rookie, and he improved those numbers to 32 catches for 772 yards and four touchdowns in

1966. Jefferson's output dropped a bit to 29 receptions for 459 yards and four scores in 1967, but his final two years with the Steelers were by far the best in his career. Jefferson tallied 58 catches for 1,074 yards and 11 touchdowns in 1968 and added 67 receptions for 1,079 yards and nine scores in 1969 to earn Pro Bowl and first-team All-Pro honors.

"Noll wouldn't tolerate bad attitudes, so he only brought in good people, as well as good football players," Steelers outside linebacker Andy Russell said. "But if you didn't have a good attitude, he'd fire you. He fired our MVP from 1969, Roy Jefferson, who was a really talented wide receiver and a good guy.

"I guess he was breaking some rules, although I don't know the whole story, so they traded him to the Baltimore Colts. Noll worked for Don Shula with the Colts, so he learned a lot from him and also playing for Paul Brown. And he took those experiences with him to the Steelers and his first head coaching job."

Jefferson wouldn't label himself as a rabble-rouser, but he admitted that there were certain things he did during his Steelers career that might have led some to believe that he could be a trouble-maker. He preferred to describe himself as a "happy-go-lucky" guy, and by all accounts that was true.

"I guess I did a lot of little things to irk Chuck, like parking in the spaces where the coaches parked, maybe being out past curfew a little too often, but I didn't feel like I had any problems on the field," Jefferson said. "But you know that coaches don't like being questioned. I know the game, and I know what I'm supposed to do. And I asked questions about things when I wanted to better understand what we were doing, but that's what they call talking back.

"So, I guess I talked back to them. At least, that's how he viewed my situation. He believed I was questioning his authority, when all I wanted to do was find out why we were doing what we were doing on offense. And don't forget, it was his first year as a head coach, so this worried him. But I can understand that. [But] I think he really had to talk Dan Rooney into getting rid of me. I think he probably went to Dan and said that I was a detriment to our team."

Jefferson also was the Steelers player-representative during a brief work stoppage during the summer, but the NFL owners eventually recognized the NFL Players Association as a representative of the players, and a collective bargaining agreement was reached.

"I was the guy who kept everybody out," Jefferson said. "Only Bobby Walden, the punter, crossed the picket line. So, I don't know. I guess that could have had something to do with it. Was I mad when I got traded? I don't know. I'll ask my wife, Candie. . . . She says I definitely was an angry man.

"But I do know that I didn't understand it. [And] I knew it wasn't because of my ability, even though Chuck made a statement when I was traded that I hadn't reached my potential, even though I led them in receiving for two seasons, made the Pro Bowl and was a first-team All-Pro in 1969."

Throughout a lengthy interview with Jefferson, he continually expressed how much he loved Pittsburgh, the people he met, and teammates who befriended him. So, Jefferson's five seasons with the Steelers were largely enjoyable, despite their abrupt end and consistent losing by the team. The Steelers were 2-12 during his rookie season and followed that with a solid 5-8-1 record in 1966. But that was the apex for victories, as the Steelers went 4-9-1 in 1967, 2-11-1 in 1968 and a resounding 1-13 in 1969.

"I enjoyed my time in Pittsburgh, on and off the field," Jefferson said. "I have never duplicated the neighborhood that

I was in, the Point Breeze area in Pittsburgh, and I knew everybody within a 2-3 square block radius there and maybe even farther. We were right off Homewood, and we knew a lot of people in Homewood, too.

"You just knew everybody, and we were all friends. Here, [in Annandale, Virginia] I might know the people on either side of me, but I never really got to know the whole neighborhood in any given situation. So, it was a more family friendly, family enjoyment type of thing in Pittsburgh than it was for us here [in the Washington, D.C. area]."

Jefferson, who will turn 70 on November 9, 2013, and his wife, Candie, already had one child when the couple arrived in Pittsburgh. Marshall Jefferson was born in Salt Lake City, while the couple attended the University of Utah. Daughter Michelle was born in Pittsburgh.

"I remember driving to the hospital at 2 or 3 o'clock in the morning and praying that my daughter would wait to arrive until we got there," Jefferson said. "She's rarely late for anything now, but I'm grateful that she didn't make an early appearance back then."

The Jeffersons had a second son, Damion, a year after Roy retired from the NFL. Michelle has a daughter, and Damion has three young children, so the Jeffersons proudly spoil four grandchildren. With such a large crew, it's obvious that family is important to them, and since the organization was run like a family, it's one of the reasons Roy was thrilled to get drafted by the Steelers.

"The Chief, he was the best," Jefferson said. "Even after I was traded, he'd send Christmas cards. He never forgot. He always asked about my kids. So, even though our seasons weren't successful seasons, I enjoyed my time in Pittsburgh. There were a lot of good people there. So, going to Pittsburgh after being at Utah was a good experience for me and my entire family. My wife loved it there, and it was a great place to begin my NFL career."

Thanks to his scholastic success as an athlete, Jefferson had several college opportunities coming out of Compton High School in California. He had his heart set on UCLA, but that dream was shattered by a 2.7 grade point average. Jefferson explained that while out-of-state students still could be eligible to attend a college in California despite a lower GPA, the state's residents needed to attend a junior college first if they didn't have a 3.0 or better.

"I guess they'd rather get the out-of-state tuition," Jefferson said. "But I did what I needed to do. I went to Compton Junior College, got the necessary grades and got into UCLA. I stayed there about a week during summer football camp, and they had me playing defensive back, wide receiver, running back and returning kicks. I didn't necessarily care where I played, but I wanted to stick with one position if that was possible."

A former Compton High School teammate, wideout Marv Fleming—who became a multiple Super Bowl winner with the Green Bay Packers and Miami Dolphins—already attended Utah. Jefferson already had visited him there, liked what he saw and decided to join Fleming.

"And I'm glad that I made that decision," Jefferson said. "Ray Nagel was the head coach. We went to the Liberty Bowl my senior year and beat West Virginia, 32-6, indoors in Atlantic City (December 19, 1964). I remember reading the paper when we came into town that we didn't have a chance, and we loved that. We dominated them right away."

Considered among the top-10 greatest games in the school's football history, Utah (8-2) had a chance to make history in the national spotlight. This was the first major college bowl game played indoors, the first broadcast nationwide in the United States and first played in Atlantic City. The game moved there and was played indoors at a temperature of 60 degrees because previous matchups took place in Philadelphia under freezing conditions. Utah stormed to a 25-0 lead through three quarters, but Jefferson—who kicked first-half field goals from 32 and 35 yards—didn't make it that far.

"I had caught three or four balls and kicked two field goals, but on the last play or so in the first half Paul Martha's brother, a safety on the WVU team, came down on me and dislocated my shoulder," Jefferson said. "So, I didn't even get to play in the second half. I spent the entire second half with my shoulder taped up and my arm in a sling."

Richie Martha, a Pittsburgh native, played for the Mountaineers. His brother, Paul, matriculated to Pitt and was a 1964 first-round NFL Draft pick by his hometown Steelers. The older Martha played for them from 1964-69 and ironically would be Jefferson's teammate during that time. Jefferson also was a No. 1 pick by the Steelers, but he was taken in the second round in 1965. The Steelers did not have a first-round pick and also traded away their selections in rounds 3-6. Jefferson was the 18th overall pick in the 1965 NFL Draft.

The New York Giants had the No. 1 overall selection and chose Auburn running back Tucker Frederickson, while North Carolina fullback Ken Willard went to the San Francisco 49ers at No. 2. The Chicago Bears acquired the third overall pick from the Steelers and chose Illinois linebacker Dick Butkus. Kansas halfback Gale Sayers went to the Bears at No. 4 and California quarterback Craig Morton to the Dallas Cowboys at No. 5. The Bears also acquired the sixth overall pick from Washington and took Tennessee offensive lineman Steve

DeLong, but he eventually signed with the San Diego Chargers in the American Football League.

The 8-10-team AFL ran in direct competition with the NFL throughout the 1960s, so the NFL franchises tried to make it extremely difficult for the AFL teams to do business. A key area to control would be the annual draft for college players that helped the league fill out its rosters. Since Jefferson was among the hot commodities coming out of Utah in 1965, the NFL sequestered him and a number of other draft-eligible players from a handful of colleges in Utah, including BYU, Utah State, and the University of Utah.

"I had no clue what I was getting into, but they had all the players stay in a hotel for the draft," Jefferson said. "They kept us there so the AFL people couldn't sign us. I agreed to sign with the Steelers and would get a $15,000 bonus check. That would allow me to pay off my little blue Ford Mustang that I had just bought. The San Diego Chargers, the reigning AFL champions, also drafted me. Even though San Diego was only 125 miles from my house, I didn't want to go anywhere else but to the NFL to play for the Steelers.

"You won't believe this, but Chuck Noll was the Chargers assistant coach who basically recruited me to sign with them. Nobody knew if the league would make it on its own or merge with the NFL, which it officially did in 1970, but they made me one heck of an offer. After the Liberty Bowl, Chuck was waiting at the hotel when we got back there. He said he had [head coach] Sid Gillman on the telephone and that he had been waiting to talk with me for an hour."

Since this was the heyday for the AFL with hot-shot players joining its teams, the Chargers offered Jefferson more than he could dream. The No. 1 pick in the AFL Draft that year was

Alabama quarterback Joe Namath, who signed with the New York Jets for a pro football record $427,000. He was a late first-round pick by the St. Louis Cardinals in the NFL Draft that year, but never played for them. Jefferson's total compensation package was quite lucrative as well.

"I was offered a $200,000 signing bonus, $20,000 a year for a two-year contract, a down payment on a house and cars for me and my wife," Jefferson said. "I also had 12-13 units left for my degree at Utah, which I eventually completed in 1968, but they said they would pay for that. And then, they wanted to pay me $125 a week just for speaking engagements and clubs and charity events and things like that. All of that . . . I couldn't believe it, but I couldn't do anything because I had already agreed to sign with the Steelers.

"And I never regretted going to Pittsburgh. I enjoyed the people on and off the field. We did a lot of charity events, working with the hospitals, local DJs, and conducting bowling tournaments. We did that more than golf events. Now, there's more golf involved, but we did a lot of bowling back then. And we had charity basketball games in the offseason against teachers from high schools in the area. Those were a lot of fun. Dick Hoak was our point guard. He could really play, a good shooter and ball-handler. So, that was a lot of fun."

Before Jefferson arrived in Pittsburgh, he had a chance to play on a senior college all-star team, and back in the day that group played a game against the reigning NFL champions. That year, it was the Cleveland Browns, who stomped the Baltimore Colts, 27-0, in the championship game. The Browns were led by Pro Bowl players in quarterback Frank Ryan, running back Jim Brown, wideout Paul Warfield, linebacker Jim Houston, and defensive linemen Dick Modzelewski and Bill Glass. And Jefferson couldn't wait to get a shot at them.

"I told my boys that I was going to put my hand in his chest and put him down if I got a shot to tackle the great Jim Brown," Jefferson said, noting that he was a college all-star as a defensive back. "There was one play, early in the game, when Brown was coming around the end. And I was coming up to make a hit. Brown was hollering at his lineman [offensive guard John] Wooten. 'Get that man, Wooten.' And Wooten blocked the linebacker. So, I had a shot at him.

"It was just me and Jim Brown. But the vicious tackle that I was going to put on Jim Brown turned into a weak body block. Every time he took a step toward me, it looked like he grew a foot. So, when we finally met, he was huge, and I threw a weak body block in there. But I caught him around the knee and got him down. He went down, but it was no vicious tackle. And he probably gained 8-9 yards, so I didn't do much more than stop him from getting a first down."

The Chargers wanted Jefferson to be a defensive back, while the Steelers didn't know what they wanted him to do. Jefferson played both ways as a rookie for the Steelers, taking some shots at receiver as well as in the secondary. And he started the final two preseason games as a receiver, but when it came time for the regular season-opener at home Jefferson got a huge surprise.

"They brought in a guy from the Canadian League to play, and they didn't even tell me about it," Jefferson said. "I thought I was going to be introduced as the starting receiver, but they called this other guy's name. You talk about being deflated. That hurt my heart. So, it was a tough first season in Pittsburgh, but things got better as we went along. And I got a lot more snaps.

"[And] I never went into any season believing it would be that bad. I really felt like we could do it, but I guess I didn't do a very good job judging our capabilities back then. I just never felt like we were going to lose when we went out there, even though we lost more often than not. Still, I enjoyed the team and the players. Andy Russell, Ray Mansfield, they were good people.

"There were a lot of other guys I became friends with during my years there," Jefferson added. "That group included Brady Keys, Ben McGee, Chuck Hinton, Joe Greene, L.C. Greenwood, Sam Davis, Marv Woodson, Cannonball Butler, Ray May, and Mike Taylor. Those were the key guys, as far as I was concerned, during my time with the Steelers."

Buddy Parker's coaching style, ignoring the draft and eschewing young players for washed-up veterans, apparently had worn thin by 1965. He was let go in the preseason, and Mike Nixon was brought in to be the head coach for just one season, and then Bill Austin was hired from 1966-68. Neither was successful.

"I don't know what the problem was, but we shuffled players in and out as much as we did head coaches back then," Jefferson said. "That was especially true at quarterback. I think Ed Brown started off as our quarterback, maybe Bill Nelson, but then there was a litany of quarterbacks after that."

Jefferson's fortunes changed dramatically when Dick Shiner came over from the Cleveland Browns after the 1967 season. He played for the Steelers from 1968-69 and completed about 47 percent of his passes for 3,278 yards and 25 touchdowns with 27 interceptions. He was sacked 57 times, but these two seasons were by far the best during his 11-year NFL career (1964-74). And they were Jefferson's best as well. The two obviously quickly developed a chemistry on the field, and the Steelers found a new superstar.

Pro-Bowl player Gary Ballman led the Steelers with 40 catches in 1965, but four players had more receptions than Jefferson's 13 as a rookie. Tight end John Hilton (46) and Ballman (41) were targeted more often than Jefferson (32 catches) in 1966, and his production dropped to 29 receptions in 1967. J.R. Wilburn and Dick Compton led the Steelers with 51 and 42 catches, respectively, that year. Hilton was fourth, behind Jefferson, with 26. The Steelers had four players with at least 20 catches in 1968, but Jefferson led the way with 58 for 1,074 yards (18.5 per catch) and 11 touchdowns. In 1969, Shiner and Terry Hanratty shared the quarterback duties, but Jefferson continued to blossom. He tallied 67 catches for 1,079 yards and nine scores to earn a second straight Pro Bowl performance and first-team All-Pro status.

"They wouldn't let me play much that first season," Jefferson said. "But Bobby Layne, who was an assistant coach with the Steelers [from 1964-65], told me something during training camp my rookie season. He said, Jefferson, if you do things right, you're going to be a great receiver in this league. I don't know why he picked me out, but I really appreciated that. Coming from a guy like him, that really meant a lot to me."

The Steelers continued to make changes to their roster and coaching staff during Jefferson's tenure, and he eventually got a chance to play for Noll when the Steelers named him their head coach in 1969. Noll, you'll recall, was Sid Gillman's defensive coordinator with the San Diego Chargers from 1962-65, and he attempted to get Jefferson to sign with the AFL's Chargers. Noll also was the defensive coordinator with head coach Don Shula and the Baltimore Colts from 1966-68. After one season together with the Steelers, Noll surprisingly sent his best player, Jefferson, to the Colts.

"The thing we had in Baltimore was Johnny Unitas, and he distributed the ball so well," Jefferson said. "We won the Super Bowl in 1970, and I had 40-some catches [44 for

749 yards and seven touchdowns]. I worked well together with Johnny, staying after practice and working hard with him. But that was it. That was my only season in Baltimore. Early on, I went to Carol Rosenbloom and said I didn't feel I should have to play under my Pittsburgh contract.

"I wanted to renegotiate. He said it would be no problem, but at the end of the season he didn't remember that conversation. So, I asked to be traded to either the West Coast teams or Washington or I would go be a teacher, because I wasn't going to play for him. I won't play for a liar. So, that's how I ended up with the Washington Redskins and head coach George Allen. He'll take a veteran over a young guy every time. That situation worked for me this time."

Jefferson held out for a short time before the Colts' training camp with Bubba Smith, the overall No. 1 pick for the Colts in 1967, but the Pro Bowl defensive end didn't last long. He went to training camp after just a couple days, while Jefferson stayed at his apartment. Eventually, the Colts tracked down Jefferson and worked out a trade with the Redskins for wide receiver Charles Wayne "Cotton" Speyrer, the club's second-round pick that year.

Jefferson spent the remainder of his 12-year NFL career with the Redskins, but neither of his six seasons in Washington was comparable to his final two with the Steelers. He recorded more than 40 receptions four out of the six seasons, but his best two were 1971-72. Jefferson tallied 44 catches for 749 yards and seven touchdowns in 1971 and added 47 for 701 yards and four scores in '72. Jefferson's 12-year totals are 451 catches for 7,539 yards (16.7 average) and 52 touchdowns. He was a true deep threat during his NFL tenure.

Some believe that Jefferson and Charley Taylor, the Redskins' top receiver before they were teammates, were at odds. Sure, Taylor's production dropped off once Jefferson arrived. He never had less than 40 catches in a season from 1964-70 with 70 or more receptions three times. Taylor tallied 72 catches for 1,119 yards and 12 touchdowns in 1966, 70 for 990 and nine scores in 1967 and 71 for 883 and eight scores in 1969. In 1971, when Jefferson joined the Redskins, Taylor played just six games. He played only 10 the year before, so Jefferson was brought in for insurance. But Taylor missed two games during his final five seasons. And they were in his final season in 1977.

"Charley Taylor and I were pretty decent friends, but he was the man," Jefferson said. "And when I got there, he wasn't the man any more. So, I think it was kind of intimidating for him, but I didn't worry about that. I didn't come in expecting anything. I just wanted to be part of the situation. I just wanted a chance. I didn't want to come in and take over, but I think it was the attitude that he thought I was carrying. And any of the guys on that team, or any of my other teammates, could tell you that I wasn't that kind of guy.

"I think I made friends on each of the three teams I played for in the NFL, but I do consider myself more of a Redskin. I kept participating in the Steelers golf tournaments and other things until recently. Since the economy has slowed down, I haven't made it back there as often. I guess I still have some animosity toward Chuck Noll, but he certainly made his mark. And the way we had our confrontation, that wasn't good for either one of us, but he really deserves his just due. He basically put the Steelers on the map."

Jefferson lives in Annandale, Virginia, and he takes part in a great deal of charitable work with the Redskins alumni. Many of those events are golf tournaments, but Jefferson hasn't had a chance to improve on his 13-handicap for about four months now. He had a knee replaced in 2012 and hip-replacement surgery in 2011.

"I've been working out on a full-time basis now for a couple weeks," Jefferson said. "I've got my weight down and write down everything I eat. I almost have my full swing back, so I'll be ready to go when the weather gets really warm."

Jefferson was named a "10 for 80" honoree for the Washington Redskins in 2012, along with LaVar Arrington, Bobby Beathard, Joe Bugel, Terry Hermeling, Jon Jansen, Richie Petitbon, Clinton Portis, Chris Samuels, and Sean Taylor. The group joined the 70 Greatest Redskins, who were named in 2002, to complete the 80 Greatest Redskins of All-Time.

In 2007, in conjunction with their 75th anniversary celebration, the Steelers named a Legends Team that included the franchise's best players from the pre-1970 era. Jefferson was a wide receiver on that team, along with quarterback Bobby Layne, running backs Dick Hoak and John Henry Johnson, wideout Ray Mathews, tight end Elbie Nickel, center Chuck Cherundolo, offensive guards Mike Sandusky and Bruce Van Dyke, and offensive tackles Charlie Bradshaw and Frank Varrichione on offense. Defensively, the tackles were Eugene "Big Daddy" Lipscomb and Ernie Stautner, the ends were Ben McGee and Bill McPeak, the linebackers were Dale Dodrill, Myron Pottios and Jerry Shipkey, and the defensive backs were Jack Butler, Bill Dudley, Howard Hartley, and Clendon Thomas. The specialists included place-kicker Armand Niccolai and punter Pat Brady.

"Both the Redskins and the Steelers took care of me and my family for those celebratory weekends," Jefferson said. "They got us there and put us up in hotels, but I shouldn't be surprised. They are two classy organizations."

That's why no one should be too surprised that Jefferson was able to fit in so well with the other players for both franchises.

Turning the Corner

The Steelers didn't trade as many draft picks late in the 1960s, the way they did every season since debuting in 1933, and there were a few players along the way who survived player purges that culminated in Chuck Noll's hiring as head coach in 1969.

West Virginia running back Dick Leftridge was the third overall pick in the first round by the Steelers during the 1966 NFL Draft, and he played just four games. Leftridge had eight carries for 17 yards and two touchdowns in his only season. In the seventh round that year, the Steelers took running back Emerson Boozer from Maryland Eastern Shore. He never made the team, but that wasn't the end of Boozer's NFL career. He moved on to the New York Jets that year and played for 10 solid seasons. Boozer tallied 5,135 yards rushing in his career (4.0 average) with 52 touchdowns. He also caught 139 passes for 1,488 yards and 12 more scores. Boozer's best season was in 1973 when he ran for 831 yards (4.6 average) and three touchdowns in 13 games. He also caught 22 passes for 130 yards and three receiving scores.

The Steelers traded their first-round choice in 1967 and chose San Diego State running back Don Shy in the second round. He spent two nondescript seasons with the Steelers and ran for 341 yards (3.4 per carry) and four touchdowns as a rookie. Shy also played for the Chicago Bears from 1970-72 and finished his career with the St. Louis Cardinals in 1973. His best season was 1971 when he ran for 420 yards and two touchdowns. The Steelers also brought in TCU quarterback Kent Nix that year, and he played for the club from 1967-69. Offensive guard Bruce Van Dyke from Missouri also came on board and was a stalwart up front from 1967-73. Nix played 25 games with the Steelers and was on the field extensively during his first season. He threw for 1,587 yards and eight touchdowns with 19 interceptions. He threw for just 1,010 yards, six touchdowns and 14 interceptions in the final two combined years. Nix finished his career with the Chicago Bears (1970-71) and Houston Oilers (1972), but he could not come close to matching the production he had during his initial season with the Steelers. Van Dyke began his NFL career in 1966 with the Philadelphia Eagles, but he was among the most popular Steelers during his time there. He played 95 games for the Steelers and then played his final 29 games with the Green Bay Packers to cap an 11-year career.

The 1968 NFL Draft had the Steelers with the 10th overall pick in the first round, and they chose Southern Cal offensive tackle Mike Taylor. After two seasons and 23 games in Pittsburgh, Taylor played two years for the New Orleans Saints (1969-70) and one with the St. Louis Cardinals (1973) to end his career. The Steelers picked Notre Dame running back Rocky Bleier in the 16th round in 1968 and also brought in Maryland quarterback Dick Shiner and Georgia punter Bobby Walden that year. Bleier and Walden were among the five players who lasted from the late 1960s, before Noll arrived, into the '70s and the Super Bowl teams.

Walden was a rookie with the Minnesota Vikings in 1964 and spent 14 seasons in the NFL, including the final 10 with the Steelers (1968-77). Walden, who won two Super Bowl rings with the Steelers, averaged nearly 42 yards per punt and had just two blocked in 974 attempts. Walden actually began his pro football career in Canada, where he played for three seasons (1961-63) and led the CFL in punting, rushing, and receiving for the Edmonton Eskimos during the final two years. Walden also led the NFL in punting in 1964 with a 46.4-yard average and was selected to the Pro Bowl after the 1969 season. In 1958, as a sophomore at Georgia, Walden led the nation in average yards per punt. As a senior in 1960, he set an Orange Bowl record for yards per punt.

The Bleier story is nothing short of amazing. It began in 1968 and after a brief hiatus, resumed in 1971 and ran until 1980. After an average three seasons at Notre Dame, with a drop-off in production as a senior, there were 416 players taken ahead of him in the 1968 NFL Draft. He played in 10 games for the Steelers as a rookie and ran for 39 yards on just six carries (6.5 average). He also had three catches for 68 yards, but did not score a touchdown. Bleier's life changed dramatically in 1969. He was drafted again, only this time by the U.S. Army, and sent to fight in the Vietnam War. On August 20, 1969, instead of sweating at training camp for first-year head coach Chuck Noll, Bleier was sloshing through rice paddies in Southeastern Asia. Later that day, Bleier's platoon was under heavy attack. The result was catastrophic.

During the fire-fight, Bleier was shot and wounded in his left leg. A grenade also exploded near him, and shrapnel littered his right leg. Bleier was awarded a Purple Heart for his injury and a Bronze Star for courageous service, but that wouldn't be his biggest accomplishment. After surgery on his legs, doctors said that he'd be lucky to walk, let alone play football again. Most people would take this as a sign, but Bleier looked at it as a challenge. He rehabbed the injuries and did not play in the NFL in 1970, but returned to the Steelers in 1971 and played just six games. Considering his strength and conditioning issues, as well as his weight loss, it's remarkable that they used him at all. He played all 14 games in 1972 and 12 in '73, primarily as a blocker and special teams ace, but Bleier's role with the Steelers altered again in 1974. A rigorous offseason training regimen boosted his weight some 30 pounds to about 212, and his attitude changed, along with his body type. The Steelers noticed.

Noll was looking for a player to join third-year running back Franco Harris in the backfield, and Bleier eventually got the call. His blocking was never in question, as Bleier continually helped open holes for Harris, but he also became an offensive threat. Bleier ran for 373 yards in 1974 and improved that total to 528 in 1975 with two touchdowns each season. But in 1976, after the Steelers had won back-to-back Super Bowls, Bleier put his name in the records book. He ran for 1,036 yards (4.7 average) and five touchdowns and combined with Harris to become just the second NFL backfield to have two 1,000-yard rushers. Miami's Larry Csonka and Mercury Morris were first, but they had to review the film after the season to get Morris to 1,000 yards.

Bleier never ran for that many yards again, but he caught 52 passes during his final two seasons with the Steelers and had a key touchdown catch in the club's 35-31 Super Bowl win against the Dallas Cowboys to cap the 1978 season.

Plagued with more than 30 years of losing, just eight winning seasons in the previous 36 and three playoff appearances, the Steelers were hopeful that another coaching change would help them finally turn things around. Chuck Noll's first draft pick in 1969 was "Mean" Joe Greene, a powerful defensive tackle from North Texas State. There were three players taken ahead of him in the NFL Draft that year, including O.J. Simpson by the Buffalo Bills with the No. 1 overall pick, but none meant as much to a franchise as Greene to the Steelers from 1969-81. The Steelers also selected Notre Dame quarterback Terry Hanratty with the first of two second-round picks, and he played for them from 1969-75. Massive Jon Kolb from Oklahoma State anchored the Steelers offensive line from 1969-81, and L.C. Greenwood was a steal in the 10th round. Greenwood, a defensive end from Arkansas AM&N, joined Greene as two members of the Steel Curtain from 1969-81.

THE EMPEROR'S NEW TEAM

The Steelers' ascent among the NFL's elite actually began in the late 1960s with a change in coaches once again and also an altered approach to the NFL Draft. Charles Henry "Chuck" Noll, 37, was hired January 27, 1969 and deftly assembled a staff that would emphasize building the current team, as well as future ones, through the annual NFL Draft. Noll ended up "presiding" over the Steelers nation for 23 seasons as the franchise's head coach, so the late Myron Cope—the team's longtime commentator—dubbed him the "Emperor."

A University of Dayton grad, Noll was a messenger guard with the Cleveland Browns for legendary head coach Paul Brown from 1953-59. He quickly got into coaching with the Los Angeles-San Diego Chargers the year after he retired as a player, first as the defensive line coach (1960-62) and then as the defensive coordinator and secondary coach (1962-65) for head coach Sid Gillman. Noll also was the defensive coordinator and secondary coach for the Baltimore Colts and head coach Don Shula (1966-68). All three head coaches that Noll worked for are enshrined in the Pro Football Hall of Fame. Noll joined them in 1993 after leading the Steelers among the NFL elite in just five seasons. Noll coached the franchise from 1969-91 and won four Super Bowls in six years (1974-79).

"Buddy Parker was a real good coach, but he had (issues)," Art Rooney Jr. said. "Then, we brought in Chuck Noll, and it was a Godsend. My brother Dan offered the job to Joe Paterno, but he knew he was going to succeed Rip Engle at Penn State. So, he turned us down, and then we needed to find another coach to hire.

"Dan and my dad asked me and some other scouts who we thought would make a good hire, since we were on the road all the time and had some thoughts. I came up with two names: Chuck Noll and Chuck Knox. But Knox never stayed in one place for long. He was like Wyatt Earp, a lot of different outposts.

"So, we eventually hired Noll," Rooney Jr. added. "He was a very intellectual guy. . . . He coached in the American Football League. Noll learned from the best of the best, and he soaked in everything those guys would tell him. He learned defense from Shula, offense from Gillman, and overall strategy from Brown."

Noll will forever be linked to Brown, the head coach during his entire playing career with the Cleveland Browns, who made the Cleveland native a 20th-round draft pick in 1953. Noll retired as a player in 1959 and immediately hooked up with Gillman and the AFL's Los Angeles Chargers in 1960.

"Gillman and Noll helped the Chargers reach the title game in the old American Football League," Rooney Jr. said. "Chuck brought two things with him from the Gillman school.

The first was weight lifting, taking smaller players who still had a football frame and turning them loose in the weight room. Muscle work. The second was film study. Gillman was just nuts about it.

"Noll told me the assistant coaches would spend hours and hours, cutting and splicing and winding the film. They'd take the film sections and drop them into waste baskets, which were all tagged and separated by position. Well, one night the cleaning guy came by. The waste cans were full, you know? After that they switched to brown paper bags, all very clearly marked: Do Not Throw Away."

Steelers head coach Bill Austin's three seasons of futility ultimately aided the franchise. His 2-11-1 record in 1968 provided Noll, his assistants and scouting department with the fourth overall pick in the ensuing (1969) draft. The Steelers used that selection to take dynamic defensive tackle "Mean" Joe Greene from North Texas State. Not only would Greene develop into a Hall-of-Fame player, he was a cornerstone for arguably the best NFL defense.

Five players who attended Noll's first team meeting after the 1968 season—running back Rocky Bleier, outside linebacker Andy Russell, punter Bobby Walden, offensive guard Sam Davis, and center Ray Mansfield—survived the final player purge and lasted through the team's initial Super Bowl appearance after the 1974 season. Bleier and Davis would earn four Super Bowl rings, while Russell, Walden, and Mansfield picked up two each.

While Greene was the key to the 1969 NFL Draft, the Steelers also secured several other successful players for the franchise's future. Quarterback Terry Hanratty from Notre Dame was taken in the second round. A native of Butler, Pennsylvania, some 35 miles north of Pittsburgh, Hanratty was a solid player for the Steelers from 1969-75. Third-round pick Jon Kolb, an offensive tackle from Oklahoma State, was a stalwart at offensive tackle from 1969-81. Hanratty picked up two Super Bowl rings, while Kolb was around for four in his tenure.

Another long-time starter was drafted that year as well, as defensive end L.C. Greenwood from Arkansas AM&N was taken in the 10th round in 1969. He also earned four Super Bowl rings from 1969-81. The Steelers won in Noll's debut game, but unceremoniously followed that with 13 straight losses to earn—and make no mistake, their poor play earned it—the No. 1 overall pick in the 1970 Draft. The Steelers selected their franchise quarterback for the future in Hall-of-Famer Terry Bradshaw, an offensive cornerstone comparable to Greene on defense. Stellar drafts continued throughout the 1970s, and the Steelers' NFL franchise went from the outhouse to the penthouse with Noll setting the pace.

"I think we just felt that we were better than what our record showed," Greenwood said. "I was there from the beginning with Chuck, and it was pretty disappointing after that first game. When we won that game, the guys were pretty fired up—especially the guys who were there for a few previous years.

"They were all fired up and thought we were going to have a heckuva year and win several football games, but we didn't win another game. So, that was disappointing. Everybody was fired up because they thought we turned the corner. You could tell by how they acted and carried themselves, but things fell apart fast after that. So, that really was a disappointing time for us."

Ensuing drafts built the Steelers into an NFL dynasty that would capture an unprecedented four Super Bowls in six seasons, and their current tally of six Lombardi Trophies is more than any other NFL franchise. But it all started with Noll, who

Byron "Whizzer" White of the Pittsburgh Pirates professional football team works out at De Witt Clinton High School in the Bronx, N.Y., in 1938. *(AP Images)*

Pittsburgh Steelers defensive linemen John Schweder (68) and Ernie Stautner (70) swarm Washington Redskins running back Rob Goode (21) at Griffith Stadium in Washington. *(AP Images)*

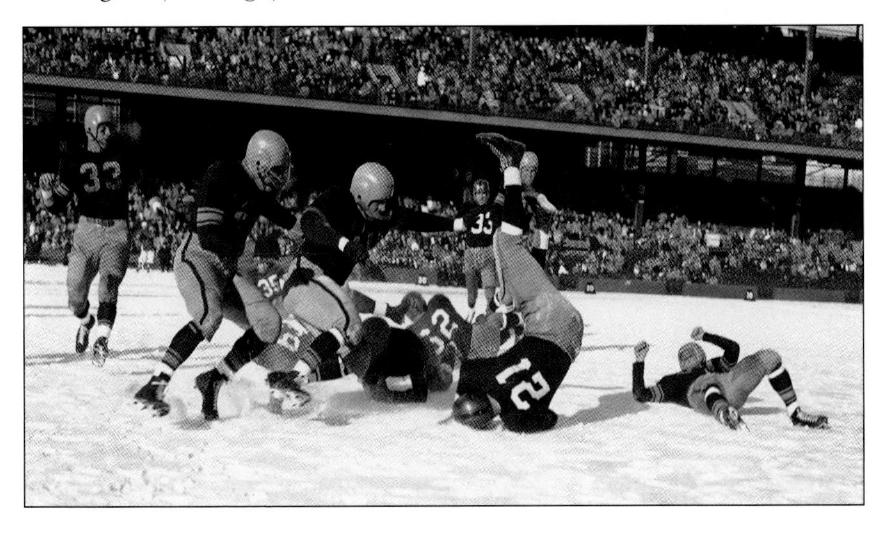

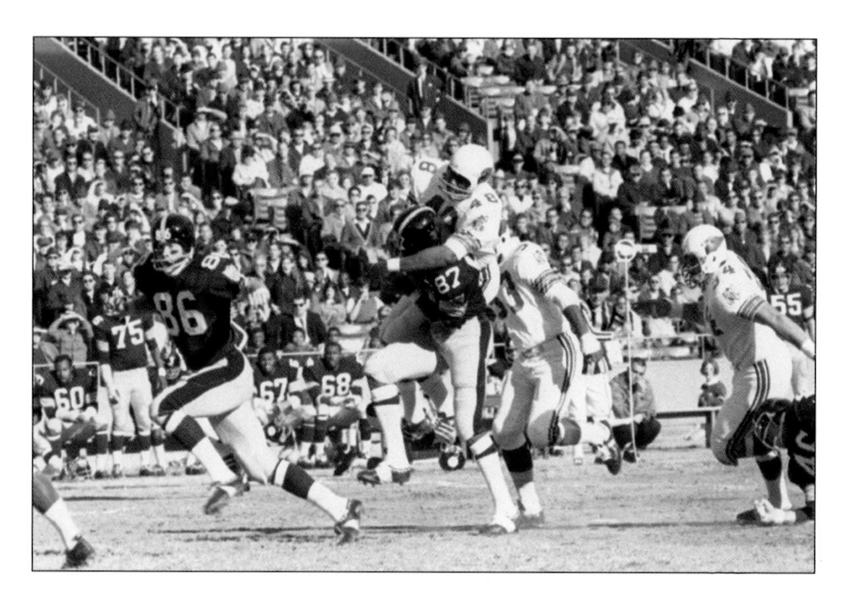

Pittsburgh Steelers wide receiver Roy Jefferson (87) catches a pass before getting hit by St. Louis Cardinals defensive back Bob Atkins (48). *(AP Images)*

Pittsburgh Steelers coach Chuck Noll, left, and quarterback Terry Bradshaw discuss strategy at a practice prior to Super Bowl XIV. *(AP Images)*

Defensive tackle "Mean" Joe Greene was the unquestioned leader of the Steel Curtain defense. *(AP Images)*

NFL commissioner Pete Rozelle, left, presents The Vince Lombardi trophy to beloved owner Art Rooney Sr. after the Pittsburgh Steelers defeated the Minnesota Vikings in Super Bowl IX. *(AP Images)*

Pittsburgh Steelers Mel Blount (47), Joe Greene (75) and Andy Russell (34) leave the field after stuffing the Minnesota Vikings in Super Bowl IX at Tulane University Stadium in New Orleans. *(AP Images)*

Pittsburgh Steelers running back Walter Abercrombie (34) runs to daylight against the Raiders at the Los Angeles Memorial Coliseum. *(AP Images/Ben Leibenberg)*

Pittsburgh Steelers running back Tim Worley (38) tries to escape the shoestring tackle of Denver Broncos free safety Dennis Smith. *(AP Images/Ben Liebenberg)*

Pittsburgh Steelers wide receiver Hines Ward (86) picks up additional yardage in a home game against the San Francisco 49ers. *(AP Images)*

Quarterback Ben Roethlisberger uncorks a pass for the Pittsburgh Steelers. *(AP Images)*

Strong safety Troy Polamalu (43) sets the Pittsburgh Steelers defense during a game against the Eagles in Philadelphia. *(AP Images/Brian Garfinkel)*

Center Maurkice Pouncey (53) provides protection for Pittsburgh Steelers quarterback Ben Roethlisberger during a home game against the Kansas City Chiefs. *(AP Images)*

Defensive end Aaron Smith shows the Pittsburgh Steelers' status after beating the Arizona Cardinals in Super Bowl XLIII. *(AP Images)*

became the franchise's 14th head coach in 1969. In just four years, Noll transformed the Steelers from the NFL's lovable losers, the same old Steelers (SOS), to a team that won the franchise's first playoff game in 1972.

"We had a bunch of guys where Chuck stirred the pot to get the guys that he wanted on the Steelers, and they were a group that had a winning attitude," Greenwood said. "We wanted to win football games, and we didn't talk about losing games. That was all in the past. So, the attitude was much better, and everybody was very disappointed when we lost a football game.

"It was more disappointing to the players than it was to the coaches, and the city actually got a winning attitude as well. We weren't the same old Steelers anymore. So, guys went out to try to improve themselves. There were more after-practice workouts, early workouts, and everybody was in the film room and weight room for extra work. It was really something.

"Once a few started it, then the whole team really picked it up," Greenwood added. "And the more successful we got, the more wins we produced, the more the city wanted. But that was fine with us, because we wanted to have winning seasons and would work hard to attain that. Chuck really did a great job by instilling that winning attitude, basically, in the entire team."

Under Noll's direction, the Steelers became the Team of the Decade in the 1970s. After going 5-9 in 1970 and 6-8 in 1971, the Steelers forged a winning record in nine straight seasons. They were 14-2 in 1978 and finished first in the AFC Central Division seven times in eight seasons. Super Bowls came after the 1974-75 seasons and 1978-79.

"Not really to brag, but I don't think there were any teams in the league at that time who were as good as we were," Greenwood said. "Sure, there were times when we didn't play up to our capabilities and got beat, but maybe the ball just didn't bounce the way that we wanted it to bounce or we just didn't play good.

"But when we went out to play, you could just tell that we were going to win the football game. You could see it during the week leading up to the game. It was all about attitude. We were physically fit to do it, and we were prepared for it. So, when you have that and the right attitude, you are going to be successful. And our opponents knew there was nothing they could do about it."

The 1980s weren't as kind to Noll and the Steelers, as they won just two playoff games in the decade and qualified for the post-season just four times overall. From 1985-88, the Steelers were the worst that they had been in some two decades with just one winning season, and they were 26-37 overall in that four-year span. Their best record was 10-6 in 1983, but the Steelers also had a low point with a 5-11 mark in 1988. It was their least amount of wins since Noll took over and went 1-13 in his debut season in 1969.

"Chuck was with us 22 years, and we didn't have a losing season for 12 straight years," Rooney Jr. said. "Everyone said it was so bad in the 1980s, but we only had three losing seasons and went to the playoffs four times. But nothing compared to the 1970s. There was limited success from the beginning to the '60s. It took Chuck a few years to get rolling, but once we did it was great.

"Chuck retired after the 1991 season, and it's interesting to me that he never did anything else, got on TV or anything like that. There's a guy writing a book on him, so maybe everyone else will get to know the guy we all know. Chuck was a no-nonsense guy. He never had throwaway lines. He always got right to the point, and you always knew where you stood with him."

Noll was forced to abdicate his throne following the 1991 season, so the Steelers needed a new leader. And while William Laird Cowher might eventually join Noll in the Pro Football Hall of Fame, he never matched the Emperor's level of success during his tenure from 1992-2006.

CHAPTER 5

The 1970s

HEADS OR TAILS? YOU MAKE THE CALL

There's no telling how the Pittsburgh Steelers fortunes would have turned had that fateful coin flip landed on heads in a New Orleans hotel in January 1970. And instead of selecting Louisiana Tech quarterback Terry Bradshaw with their first-round pick, the Steelers could have had Purdue's Mike Phipps, San Diego State's Dennis Shaw, Florida State's Bill Cappleman, North Texas State's Steve Ramsey, Oklahoma State's Bob Cutburth, Houston's Rusty Clark, Iowa's Mike Cilek, Davidson's Gordon Slade, U.S. International's Wayne Clark, Southern Cal's Mike Holmgren, Hawaii's Larry Arnold or Northern Arizona's Bob Stewart.

However, after decades of struggles on and off the field, poor coaching, and bad players, the Steelers finally made the right decision. Sure, they made a good call by selecting Chuck Noll to be the head coach in 1969 and taking Joe Greene with the fourth overall pick in the first round later that year, but this decision was a little different. With identical 1-13 records in 1969, the Steelers and Chicago Bears had to flip a coin to determine which team would get the No. 1 overall pick and ultimately select Bradshaw, the consensus best quarterback available.

The Steelers beat the Detroit Lions 16-13 in the 1969 season-opener and then lost 13 straight. Among those was a Week 8 road defeat, 38-7, to the Chicago Bears. Obviously, it was the Bears' only victory. NFL Commissioner Pete Rozelle was ready to toss the coin, and Steelers president Dan Rooney—the eldest son of team founder Art Rooney Sr.—deferred the call, on advice from his father, to Bears executive Ed McCaskey. He called heads, but the 1921 silver dollar landed on tails to elicit cheers from Rooney and Noll.

So, after dumping future Hall-of-Fame quarterbacks Johnny Unitas in 1955 before the season began and Len Dawson after three nondescript seasons (1957-59), along with 22-year NFL veteran Earl Morrall after just two seasons (1957-58), the Steelers finally had their franchise quarterback in Bradshaw. Sure, there were tremendous growing pains during the first couple seasons, but Bradshaw would help lead the Steelers to four Super Bowls in six seasons from 1974-79. And more importantly, Bradshaw eventually would follow Unitas and Dawson into the Pro Football Hall of Fame. That's not too shabby for the previous lovable-loser Steelers, but what would have happened had that coin landed on heads? Who would have been the Steelers first-round pick with the second overall selection? They still would have needed a quarterback and could have selected one of the aforementioned 12 others taken that day.

It seems that the Bears were so distraught by missing out on Bradshaw that they didn't even want the No. 2 pick, so they traded it to rival Green Bay. The Packers selected Notre Dame defensive tackle Mike McCoy. The Cleveland Browns had the No. 3 pick, acquired from the Miami Dolphins, and took Phipps. He spent seven years in Cleveland and actually ended his NFL career in 1981 after five seasons in Chicago. There were no other quarterbacks taken in the first round. Utah State defensive tackle Phil Olsen went to the Boston Patriots with the fourth overall pick, and Southern Cal defensive end Al Cowlings was taken by the Buffalo Bills at No. 5. Cowlings might be better known to some as the driver of the white Ford Bronco with passenger O.J. Simpson in a low-speed chase with police in 1994 after the murder of Simpson's wife, Nicole Brown Simpson, and her friend, Ronald Goldman.

The remaining top-10 first-round picks in 1970 were Oklahoma tight end Steve Zabel by the Philadelphia Eagles at No. 6, Penn State defensive tackle Mike Reid by the Cincinnati Bengals at No. 7, Texas A&M running back Larry Stegent by the St. Louis Cardinals at No. 8, North Texas State defensive end Cedric Hardman by the San Francisco 49ers at No. 9, and Texas Southern wide receiver Ken Burrough by the New Orleans Saints at No. 10.

Along with Bradshaw, the Steelers hit on second-round pick Ron Shanklin and had another grand slam with defensive back Mel Blount in the third round in 1970. Blount had a spectacular 14-year career with the Steelers and missed just one game from his rookie season until 1981, despite a tremendously physical style of play. Blount missed seven games in 1982, but played all 16 in 1983 before retiring as a four-time Super Bowl champion. Blount redefined cornerback play in the NFL during his tenure, which prompted rule changes to a less-physical style, and his career culminated in his enshrinement in the Pro Football Hall of Fame. Blount was the second of eight future

Hall-of-Fame performers that the Steelers drafted during the 1970s, when they were known as the Team of the Decade. Shanklin, taken in the second round in 1970, caught 147 passes for 2,723 yards (18.5 per catch) and 23 touchdowns from 1970-73. He gave the Steelers a true long-ball threat, but things changed for Shanklin. The Steelers already added Frank Lewis, their No. 1 pick in 1971, and they selected two more wide receivers in 1974, which dropped Shanklin's production to 19 catches for 324 yards and one touchdown. And even though he started in the 1974 Super Bowl, he was gone before the next season.

The Steelers made two other acquisitions for the 1970 season. They signed Morgan State running back John "Frenchy" Fuqua after one season with the New York Giants and picked up Illinois running back Preston Pearson after three seasons with the Baltimore Colts to shore up the running game. Fuqua was one of the true characters of a decade when the Steelers were filled with them. He wore a flashy cape to highlight brightly colored outfits that on one occasion included live goldfish swimming in the plexiglass heels of his shoes. He also ran for nearly 3,000 yards and 21 touchdowns in seven seasons with the Steelers from 1970-76. He was on two Super Bowl teams. Pearson played in one Super Bowl with the Steelers and two against them for the Dallas Cowboys during his 14-year NFL career. In five seasons with the Steelers (1970-74), Pearson ran for 2,243 yards and eight touchdowns to go with 59 catches and another four scores. That early stretch was the best offensive production in his career. He was more productive as a pass-catcher for the Cowboys with 189 catches and 11 touchdowns in six seasons in Dallas (1975-80).

There were two other significant changes for the Steelers in 1970. First, Three Rivers Stadium opened and was their home for three memorable decades from 1970-2000. The Steelers had played their home games at Forbes Field from 1933-57 and at both Forbes Field and Pitt Stadium from 1958-63. From 1964-69, the Steelers played at Pitt Stadium until Three Rivers opened in 1970. They shared the stadium with major league baseball's Pittsburgh Pirates. The other change occurred before the season as well, as the Steelers moved from the NFL's Century Division to the American Football Conference's Central Division with the Cleveland Browns, Cincinnati Bengals and Houston Oilers. The change occurred when the NFL merged with the American Football League (AFL). The new NFL was divided into two, 13-team conferences, the AFC and NFC (National Football Conference) with three divisions in each, the East, Central and West divisions. Each east division had five teams, while the central and west had four each in the expanded 26-team NFL.

The NFL embarked on a new era in 1970, during which the league and its franchises flourished. So, as the NFL's revenue, popularity, and success would increase markedly, the same could be said for what would become one of its premier franchises, the Pittsburgh Steelers.

Hey, What About Us?

While the Steelers' 1974 NFL Draft is lauded among the best in the league's history—and it certainly should be with four future Hall-of-Famers joining the club from Rounds 1-5—the franchise's player haul in 1971 was spectacular in its own right. The club selected seven future starters in the draft, including one future Hall-of-Famer, and signed two other starters.

"Not at all to diminish what those players accomplished from the 1974 draft, but coming out of 1972 I think that Noll had put the organization, the team, and the players' confidence over the hump," former safety Mike Wagner said. "It was just a matter of how good could we be? And the nucleus of that 1974 team that won that first championship, those players made contributions. But I think if you'll look at the roster right through that Super Bowl, those Hall of Famers from 1974 made most of their contributions following 1975 and in later years.

"I came in [as an 11th-round draft pick in] 1971 and was part of that losing legacy and attitude and just saw it turn as more and more good players were brought in. To me, that's what it was. Noll was preaching a message that he was going to put players on the field that could win. Part of it, particularly for someone like me who was a low-round draft pick, was that we were as good if not better than anybody else in the league and getting us to believe it and working toward it. Eventually, there was tangible proof on the football field in terms of wins and championships."

Grambling wideout Frank Lewis was the club's first-round pick, the eighth overall selection, and he collected two Super Bowl rings for the Steelers from 1971-77. A long-ball threat from the outset, the speedy Lewis caught 128 passes with 16 touchdowns in seven seasons for the Steelers. He also played six years for the Buffalo Bills and had increased production with two 1,000-yard seasons. Lewis' best season overall was 70 catches for 1,244 yards and four touchdowns in 1981. He tallied 397 career catches for 6,724 yards (16.9 average) and 40 touchdowns.

"If I would have received a lot of media attention and action that first year, maybe I would have felt pressure as a first round pick," Lewis said during an interview with the *Pittsburgh*

Sports Daily Bulletin. "The way you deal with pressure, competition is to be ready when your number is called. [But] the history of the team never crossed my mind. The Steelers picked me in the draft, so they were my team, regardless of the past. The receivers were first- and second-year players, so everyone was learning at the same rate.

"However, I have to say, the veterans always helped a younger player when they could. The biggest adjustment for me was not playing and waiting for the opportunity as a rookie, because coming out of Grambling my adjustments were very small. (But) I was there when the team started growing into a championship team, and from my perspective the leap began in 1972 when after so many years the Steelers won the division and just missed going to the Super Bowl with less than two minutes remaining in the championship game."

One of the best outside linebackers of all time was secured when the Steelers took Jack Ham from Penn State in the second round of the 1971 draft. He played for the Steelers from 1971-82, and made eight straight Pro Bowls with six first-team All-Pro selections. Ham played a starring role in the Steelers' four Super Bowl victories during the 1970s. Two future starters and four-time Super Bowl winners were taken in the fourth round in Gerry "Moon" Mullins, an offensive guard from Southern Cal (1971-79); and Dwight "Mad Dog" White, a defensive end from East Texas State (1971-80).

In the fifth round, the Steelers selected Kansas tight end Larry Brown. While he was drafted to be a big pass-catching target, the 6-foot-4, 250-pound Brown was more like an offensive tackle and actually played that position during the latter half of his 14-year NFL career with the Steelers. The four-time Super Bowl winner caught 48 passes for 636 yards and five touchdowns, but he eventually made the Pro Bowl as a lineman. Brown had his own thoughts why the Steelers drafted him.

"You know, the Steelers had this philosophy about drafting the best athlete available when it was their turn to pick, so I guess that's one reason why they took me," Brown said. "So, I guess they thought I had some potential, but as far as making the team there really wasn't one thing that helped me along. They needed a tight end, and I had some size and fit the profile for the position in terms of size and speed and was able to make it with the way I played.

"Chuck had a plan on how he would build the team, and that's how they did things back then. There was competition at every position, and it was always fair. It was based on a player's ability, so everybody had a chance. Some guys had more ability than others, and they were the ones who played. [Chuck's philosophy] was that you had to step up your game or he'd find someone to take your place. It was all about getting the best players on the squad, and he didn't care where those guys came from or who they were as long as they could play."

Brown was always more of a blocker than a pass-catcher, although he caught 33 passes for 434 yards and two touchdowns from 1974-75. Brown also caught a four-yard touchdown pass from Terry Bradshaw in Super Bowl IX.

"I played tight end according to the way they wanted to use a tight end on offense," Brown said. "Tight ends were essential in their running game, so they wanted a tight end who could block, but also catch passes, so my versatility was a key factor. The year I switched [to tackle], I had a knee injury, [and] I was still recovering. I wasn't able to do all the running and cutting needed to play tight end. That was anticipated by Chuck. He called me into his office, and he told me that because I couldn't run due to the injury he was going to have me learn the tackle position. And once I got healthy, I would get to move back to tight end.

"In the meantime, they drafted Bennie Cunningham in the first round and signed Randy Grossman [two tight ends]. They saw themselves as being in good shape at tight end and had great need at tackle at the same time, so they never moved me back. Then, they traded away tackle Gordon Gravelle, so I stayed at right tackle for eight years and won two more Super Bowls. I saw myself as a tight end before the move to tackle, but you have to move on at some point in your career. I was used to playing with the ball, catching and running. So I guessed I missed it, sure, but not to a point where it was difficult to get past. And with my knee issues, it made things a lot easier for me at tackle."

Brown appears to be a good-natured, happy-go-lucky guy, and the Steelers locker room was filled with pranksters in those days. But it's difficult to imagine that someone would pick on a guy who was Brown's size.

"[Quarterback Terry] Hanratty played a number of practical jokes," Brown said. "I also remember a guy . . . Dennis Hughes, who was a tight end from Georgia. He and Hanratty used to go back and forth, taking things out of each other's lockers, putting that hot gel stuff in people's shorts. They were always doing something, hiding clothes. They were serious practical jokesters.

"There was this one day when Dennis just got done getting someone with a practical joke. He was so excited that he got someone, and he was laughing so hard while walking to his locker. When he gets there, he didn't see his clothes. He just said, in that exaggerated Southern drawl: 'Dang it, someone stole my clothes.' The whole locker room was laughing like crazy. It finally occurred to Dennis that he was wearing his clothes the whole time. There were some great guys back then."

In the eighth round in 1971, the Steelers picked powerhouse defensive tackle Ernie "Fats" Holmes from Texas Southern. He earned two Super Bowl rings from 1972-77. And in the 11th round, the Steelers selected safety Mike Wagner from Western Illinois. He won four Super Bowls in his 10-year career (1971-80). The Steelers didn't draft, but signed place-kicker Roy Gerela from New Mexico State (1971-78) and hard-hitting safety Glen Edwards from Florida A&M (1971-77). Gerela won three Super Bowls, while Edwards earned two Lombardi trophies.

"I think that mentally, particularly after we got through the 1972 season—even though we lost to the undefeated Dolphins—I think the core of players and coaching staffs were convinced that we could play on any given game day as well or better than most of the other teams in the NFL," Wagner said. "And I think also, if you look at some of those games—maybe not the so-called big games—but ones that put us in a position to go into the playoffs, we had this mindset that the fourth quarter was a quarter that we would win on defense and offense. And that would be enough to push us to a win in those games.

"But I know that Noll and some of the staff used to go crazy during the 1970s. One of his locker-room speeches at halftime was when he would ask us if we believed we could turn it on and off anytime that we wanted, because he was unhappy with our first-half efforts. But there were some players on the team, not including myself, who basically had a couple different gears and switches that could make them play at a higher level. I think that sometimes we can focus too much on what play cost the game, but my attitude—and I think the attitude of most of my teammates—was that the most important play is the last play that occurs that can decide between you winning and losing.

"So, I've always been of the mindset that as long as you have a chance to win, there's still a key play that has yet to be made, whether it's knocking a pass down at the end of a game or making a key tackle or field goal or big catch or something like that," Wagner added. "So, that was always our mindset. Sure, there were some spectacular plays that keyed our victories, that's for sure, but there were also a lot of things that happened at the end of the games that were just as critical to either team's success or failure in the game."

And with players like the ones the Steelers brought in for the 1971 season and added in the future, much more success was on the way.

A New Plateau Is Reached

The Steelers 40th NFL season began with such promise in 1972, as Penn State running back Franco Harris was taken with the 13th overall pick in the first round during the annual NFL Draft. But that was just the tip of the iceberg for the Steelers, who picked up seven players who would make contributions during the next decade. Five of those players came via the draft. Along with Harris (1972-83), the Steelers secured offensive lineman Gordon Gravelle from BYU (1972-76) in the second round, Clemson tight end John McMakin in the third round (1972-74), Rhode Island defensive tackle Steve Furness in the fifth round (1972-80) and Tennessee State quarterback "Jefferson Street" Joe Gilliam in the 11th round (1972-75). The Steelers also signed Texas Southern defensive tackle Ernie "Fats" Holmes (1972-77) and Northwestern tight end-receiver

Barry Pearson (1972-73). Pearson played a small part in the most famous play in NFL history, the "Immaculate Reception" touchdown catch by Harris.

"My decision to sign with the Steelers wasn't really difficult," Pearson told the *Pittsburgh Sports Daily Bulletin*. "I had a number of teams that wanted to sign me, and I selected the Steelers because Lionel Taylor, the receivers coach, had come to Northwestern and watched me practice. [He] spent time talking to me and actually called and wanted to sign me, not some scout that I had never met. As far as making the roster, you hope you get enough opportunities to show that you belong, and I guess I accomplished that."

The Steelers had a few things to accomplish before Harris made history, and they achieved their goals by going 11-3 to win the AFC's Central Division title. Their only losses were on the road, to the Cincinnati Bengals, Cleveland Browns, and Dallas Cowboys. Olympic sprinter "Bullet" Bob Hayes scored on a halfback pass to key the close game for "America's Team," but the Steelers would get a measure of payback against the Cowboys later in the decade.

"I think 1972 was the turnaround year," Steelers outside linebacker Andy Russell said. "We drafted Franco and lost only three games during the regular season. One of those games was to Dallas, and I had to cover Bob Hayes in that game. I had deep help, sure, but my job was to jam him.

"I went to do that one time and didn't get the job done. When I came off the field, the coaches yelled at me. I told them it was physics. He runs a 9.1 100-yard dash, and I'd be lucky to run a 12.1. You can't even imagine what that feels like to run next to a guy who can run that fast. It was just incredible."

So were the Steelers that season. They reached the AFC playoffs for the first time and actually won a game at

Three Rivers Stadium, thanks to Harris and the "Immaculate Reception." In a nutshell, the Steelers held the early lead against the Oakland Raiders, 6-0, on two Roy Gerela field goals. But the soon-to-be hated Raiders took a 7-6 lead when quarterback Ken Stabler rolled out and rumbled for a 30-yard touchdown.

"We were thinking, 'This thing's over,' " Raiders linebacker Phil Villapiano recalled. "Our defense could stop them at any time. We're in the huddle, and we're pretty happy. We had set up a deep zone, and we didn't think there was any way they were going to penetrate it."

The Steelers couldn't make any progress, and it was a fourth-and-10 situation with 22 seconds remaining. It was the last gasp for Pittsburgh. Several Steelers players have said that the original play was supposed to go to Pearson, although Frenchy Fuqua believed Bradshaw had him in mind from the start.

"That pass was coming to me from the get-go," Fuqua said during the Immaculate Reception's 40th anniversary celebration in 2012. "Ron Shanklin and I had led the team in receiving the previous season [49 catches each], and I was considered one of our most sure-handed receivers. When Bradshaw went to the sideline to confer with the coaches before that play, I watched those blue eyes from the sideline to the huddle, and I knew he was going to throw the ball to me. Bradshaw eyed me all the way back to the huddle.

"If the timing had worked out, and the pass protection hadn't broken down—Otis Sistrunk nearly got Terry—I was wide open. I'd have gotten to the end zone or to the sideline, and Roy Gerela would have had an easy kick for a field goal to win it. I could have been the hero. But Bradshaw had to duck under and away from the rush. He ran to the right. Tatum left one of our wide receivers, Barry Pearson, and came up to cover me. The ball came my way."

Pearson added his rendition of the situation.

"I was the one who brought in the play," Pearson said. "The play call was half-right, split opposite 66 out end in. It was supposed to go to me, but the line broke down on the right side and forced Bradshaw to move to his left. He couldn't throw across the field, of course, so he had to throw in desperation toward Frenchy. I was wide open, too, and the play was only meant to get a first down. . . . There was plenty of time to move the ball and try to score later."

Here's the call by Jack Fleming, the Steelers play-by-play announcer, who called the game for the team's radio broadcast.

"Hang onto your hats, here come the Steelers out of the huddle. Terry Bradshaw at the controls, 22 seconds remaining. And this crowd is standing. Bradshaw back and looking again. Bradshaw running out of the pocket, looking for somebody to throw to, fires it downfield ... and there's a collision. And it's caught out of the air. The ball is pulled in by Franco Harris. Harris is going for a touchdown for Pittsburgh. Harris is going. ... Five seconds left on the clock. Franco Harris pulled in the football, I don't even know where he came from. Fuqua was in a collision. There are people in the end zone. Where did he come from? Absolutely unbelievable. Holy moly!"

Keep in mind that Fleming screamed through the entire call, and Three Rivers Stadium was shaking throughout. There was bedlam, as game officials attempted to determine if it was a legal play. The rule those days was that two offensive players couldn't touch the ball in succession, so if Frenchy Fuqua touched the ball on the initial deflection, instead of Oakland's Jack Tatum, the touchdown would not count. If Tatum touched it, the Steelers would win the game, 13-7, and move on to the AFC championship game.

"If you'd asked all the players, Pittsburgh and Oakland, I'll bet none of them knew the two-touch rule," Villapiano said. "But Coach Madden knew. He called us over, because it was getting pretty crazy out there on the field. He told us the ball can't go offense to offense, and we were thinking, 'Whoa, Coach might have them on a technicality.' We just had to wait for the decision."

That basically was up to NFL supervisor of officials Art McNally, who was in the Steelers press box, and the on-field officials called him up there to get the correct call. The Immaculate Reception took 17 seconds, but it took the officials about 15 minutes to definitively make the final call of a touchdown. To get to that point, referee Fred Swearingen called for an officials' conference.

"He called a conference, which was good to do," McNally said. "You ask them: 'What did you see?' You put it together, and you come out and just say yes or no. [But] the conference just stretched out and stretched out and stretched out. I said, 'What's the problem?' They wondered about the double-touch rule. And lo and behold, here comes the referee. He's leaving the field."

Swearingen went to the baseball dugout on the Steelers sideline and called McNally, who says that prior to his chat with Swearingen he never looked at a replay, which was not part of officiating then. He said he never told Swearingen what call to make. McNally says Swearingen told him that two members of his crew had said the ball was touched by Tatum, making it a legal catch.

"Once he said that, everything is fine," McNally said. "They made the decision. And what I said to him was, 'OK, you're fine. Go ahead and go.' That was the extent of the conversation between Fred Swearingen and myself."

McNally says, based on his view from the press box, they made the right call. He said he also learned later that Swearingen had intended to ask him what his opinion was on the play.

"He never had a chance to say it," McNally said. "It's something a referee should not do. You make the decision down there, [though] it's different with replay now. [But] I would have told him my opinion. Tatum touched the ball. I said it might have been the last thing I would have done. But I said I wouldn't have let him hang."

Many of the Raiders have said the officials were reluctant to overturn the call because they feared for their safety on the field had they nullified the Steelers' touchdown. Long-time Raiders coach John Madden still fumes about the play and won't discuss it to this day. Villapiano attended the 40th anniversary celebration, but Madden has never shown up and likely never will.

"That's a lot of baloney," McNally said, referring to Madden's contention that the officials feared for their safety.

And so the Steelers moved on to the AFC championship game for the first time, also at Three Rivers Stadium, to face the undefeated Miami Dolphins. It definitely wasn't the Steelers' time, yet, but they could have beaten the Dolphins and stopped their undefeated run to the Super Bowl. Instead, a fake punt by the Dolphins turned the game around, and the Steelers lost, 21-17.

But they were the NFL's lovable losers no more. Not only did the Steelers franchise turn the corner, it was well on its way toward an unprecedented level of success that the NFL had not seen before nor since.

Simply the Best

Sure, the Steelers were 10-4 in 1973 and finished second in the AFC Central Division, but they quickly were eliminated in the playoffs by the Oakland Raiders, who got some measure of revenge for the previous year with a 33-14 thrashing. But two future starters were secured in the draft, as Florida State cornerback J.T. Thomas was taken with the fourth overall pick during the first round, and California linebacker Loren Toews was taken in the eighth round. Thomas played for the Steelers from 1973-77 and 1979-81, while Toews was a solid performer from 1973-83. Each player collected four Super Bowl rings.

"Actually, I was sleeping when I got drafted, so I had no idea that the Steelers drafted me," Thomas said. "I didn't have an agent, but I had been in touch with a guy in Houston who showed some interest. Some other Florida State players wanted to watch the draft with this guy, but I worked my way back to Tallahassee and had a long bus ride there from Jacksonville. I got in about six in the morning, and since I couldn't sleep on the bus I was really tired.

"We had hall phones back then, and one of my FSU teammates banged on my door to tell me Coach wanted to talk to me. He wanted to know where I had been, so I told him the story. He told me to get down to the local TV station to do an interview, because I was the No. 1 pick by the Pittsburgh Steelers. I never talked with them or even heard from them before the draft. I really didn't know too much about them, either, but I believe it was kind of destined to happen."

Thomas explained that he was playing in the East-West Shrine Game after the college football season and was at a banquet leading up to the December 30, 1972, game in San Francisco. It was a week before the game, because the Steelers were playing the Oakland Raiders in an AFC playoff game December 23.

"I was with a bunch of other guys at this banquet hall where we were having a big dinner in conjunction with the game," Thomas said. "We were having a real good time, maybe 30-40 guys there, and they wanted to bet on the game. I was about the only guy who bet on the Steelers at $30 for each guy. So, it's like $900 at stake here. The Steelers took an early lead on two field goals, but the Raiders finally scored and it was getting late in the game. I really was getting worried, because I didn't have more than $200 in my pocket, if that. It's what was left from the $500 that I had when I went out there to the game.

"So, I went to leave before the game ended, and the sous chefs that they had there stopped me from leaving. They were really big guys, bigger than me, so I grabbed a chair and sat by the door. I really was getting nervous, as the time was running out real quick. All of a sudden, all the other guys were yelling and cursing, and I looked up to see Franco Harris running down the sideline for a touchdown. I couldn't believe it, but there were two sabers laying on the table for decoration, and I grabbed them. I also got a pot, stood on top of the chair by the door and started banging the pot. I must have been quite a sight.

"I told those guys that nobody was leaving until they all paid me the money that they owed me," Thomas added. "Like I said, it was like $900 that I was able to take back to Tallahassee, and I never had $900 in my life. Then, I get drafted by the Steelers, and when I got to training camp Franco picked me to be his roommate. He was just in his second season, but he already made an impact in the NFL. And he picked me to be his roommate. Can you believe that? It had to be destiny for me to be drafted by the Pittsburgh Steelers."

While Thomas and Toews were good players for a long time for the Steelers, they were just the beginning. The Steelers hit the jackpot in the 1974 NFL Draft. Four future Hall-of-Famers, along with the previous stockpiled talent on the roster, helped the Steelers set off a dominant stretch with six straight AFC Central Division titles (1974-79), a six-year record at

67-20-1, a 13-2 post-season mark and four Super Bowl trophies (1974-75, 78-79).

Southern Cal wide receiver Lynn Swann (1974-82) topped the 1974 NFL Draft for the Steelers, while Kent State linebacker Jack Lambert (1974-84) was taken in the second round. Alabama A&M wideout John Stallworth (1974-87) was the first of two fourth-round picks and the third future Hall-of-Famer selected by the Steelers, while UCLA cornerback Jimmy Allen (1974-77) was the other fourth-rounder. The fourth future Hall-of-Fame player was Wisconsin center Mike Webster (1974-88), and he was taken in the fifth round. South Carolina State safety Donnie Shell (1974-87) was signed as a free agent.

The Steelers won the first of six consecutive AFC Central titles in 1974 and rolled past Buffalo (32-14) and Oakland (24-13) on their way to Super Bowl IX. The destructive Steel Curtain defense dominated the Minnesota Vikings, and Harris ran for 158 yards and a touchdown to key a 16-6 victory. The amazing mix of veterans and young players for the Steelers were just getting started.

"We had a lot of different characters on those teams," Thomas said. "Chuck Noll relied on being a great communicator, and just about every player needed a different type of communication. For example, if Chuck communicated with Joe Greene, it was different from Terry Bradshaw. Joe needed to be heard, and Bradshaw needed to be a thrower. And Chuck knew that. As far as I was concerned, I just needed a wink and a nod. . . . He could be talking to all of us in a team meeting, and nobody knew who he was talking to exactly.

"Dwight White, he was a big talker. Actually, both of us were pretty big talkers, and we roomed together for a while. Chuck said we were perfect roommates, because we would stay up half the night talking about any number of different things. Probably nobody else would have roomed with us anyway. Mike Wagner was a very tough guy and very intelligent guy. He probably was considered to be the quarterback for the defense. He was a good communicator on the field and just a class act. He reminded me of a college professor."

Thomas described the Steelers of the 1970s as a mixed bag with numerous different personalities. On the left side, there basically was Thomas, Jack Ham, L.C. Greenwood, and Wagner. That was the strong side.

"We did what we had to do, but this group of guys probably wasn't going to start a fight with anybody," Thomas noted. On the right side, it all started up front with defensive tackle Mean Joe Greene.

"That's where the metamorphosis took place," Thomas said. "We all knew the kind of guy Joe was. He was nasty and mean, and he didn't have that moniker in name only. He was that mean, and he earned that name. I mean, if you're going down a dark alley, you needed to take Joe and Lambert with you. If you did that, you would be all right. So, when you get to Joe, the whole defense changed. Joe was just unbelievable, and he was dominant in every game. Then, there was Ernie Holmes, and God only knew what he would do.

"And Dwight was on the end. Dwight didn't trust Ernie, because he would call something and Ernie would do just the opposite. I guess he just changed his mind for some reason or another, but he would just do it. We didn't know what Ernie was doing, but he knew. And he always made the right decision. And even if the coaches complained about it, Ernie always had an explanation. It didn't make sense to anybody but Ernie, but he still tried to explain it. There was Lambert in the middle, and Glen Edwards at the other safety spot.

"Of course, Mel Blount was at the other corner spot," Thomas added. "Glen, he would try to take off somebody's head every time he got the chance. Mel, you know he owns all those horses, right? Well, he actually thought he was a horse. He was a big guy, but he could run. We had a big secondary that could run. I ran about a 4.4, and Mel probably could get to 4.2 if needed. Quarterbacks, they thought they had Mel beat, and they might have had him. But once the ball was in the air, that's when Mel made his move. He could really close on the ball."

Thomas also mentioned the other members of the Steelers 1970s Super Bowl teams. There was Andy Russell as the outside linebacker opposite Ham. Wagner eventually was moved to free safety, and Edwards was replaced by nickel back Donnie Shell. Steve Furness took over for Holmes, and Toews eventually replaced Russell as the starter, with Robin Cole also playing extensively at the position. Defensive tackle Gary Dunn, linebacker Dennis "Dirt" Winston, cornerback Ron Johnson, and defensive end John Banaszak also were key players during the latter part of the decade. Thomas wouldn't go so far as to say that the Steelers freelanced on defense, but he believed they only ran the plays that were called in the huddle maybe half the time.

"Sometimes we reacted to what was happening on the field," Thomas said. "We did things that we should have done when the offense did what it did, but that wasn't the play that was called. With the personnel that we had, that allowed us to react to what happened and get the job done no matter what. After that, the play that we actually ran, that would become an audible or another part of our defense. I'll use an example from playing the Oakland Raiders. We'd be in man-to-man coverage, and a lot of times I would have tight end Dave Casper.

"They would see me on Casper, and Ham would be outside of me because he had the back. So, they thought I would follow Casper, and he would take me outside. Then, they could blow me up with the fullback, Pete Banaszak. He was a big, strong guy and a terrific blocker. But when Casper turned outside on Ham, I went on instinct and hit the hole. I nailed the running back, Clarence Davis, in the backfield. I have no idea what made me do that, but as soon as Casper moved out on Ham I shot through the hole and made the play.

"Mel would tell you that he wrote the playbook, and he had quite a few, but that one was mine," Thomas said. "Still, there were a lot of improvisational things that we did that ended up being the regular way that we would do things. Another thing was the way Ernie and Joe would hit the gaps. They would stunt and twist all the time. You never knew what our D-line was going to do on any given play. And when they got in the gaps to occupy two guys, the offense couldn't get anybody on Lambert, and then he wreaked havoc on the back or receiver or whoever came in his area. That was devastating."

After he retired, Thomas ran into a former Dallas Cowboys defensive back who told him they tried to run the defensive plays the Steelers used so successfully.

"Can you believe that?" Thomas said. "After we kicked their butts in two Super Bowls, the Cowboys tried to do some of the things that we were doing on defense, but they couldn't do it. Then, they realized that it wasn't the plays. It was the talent, and they didn't have as much as we did on that side of the ball. That was the difference. We had speed and had size. Blount's closing speed, it was like the Roadrunner. He could shift gears and get to another level.

"It was a phenomenon. That's why we called him Supe, for Superman. He was that good. We had 11 Pro Bowl starting defensemen in Super Bowl X. The system of play was based on talent and technique much more than theory. That's why when those players retired, the playbook became useless. The coaches would record the plays to learn from them, but the Steelers couldn't duplicate it, let alone another team. Nobody could run those plays."

That's because the Steelers teams from the mid-to-late 1970s had a talent level that was unparalleled.

More of the Same

The Steelers' NFL Draft selections during the second half of the 1970s produced no future Hall-of-Famers, but there were plenty of good players who were invaluable to the franchise's continued pursuit of Lombardi trophies. And several of those players had careers that extended far into the 1980s. Their 1975 No. 1 pick was not one of them. Michigan cornerback Dave Brown was the 26th overall pick in the first round, as the Steelers chose late due to winning the Super Bowl, and he played a supporting role on the club's defensive efforts toward winning back-to-back Super Bowls. Brown also was a punt-returner for the Steelers, but his best seasons during a 15-year NFL career were not with them. He was selected in the expansion draft the next season by the Seattle Seahawks and spent the next decade with them. He set an NFL record by returning two interceptions for touchdowns in one game, made the Pro Bowl in 1984, was a two-time All-Pro (1984-85) and spent three seasons with the Green Bay Packers to end a solid career with 62 interceptions and five TD returns. Unfortunately, Brown never reached his 53rd birthday, as he died of an apparent heart attack while playing basketball with his son in 2006.

None of the Steelers' draft picks in the remaining 16 rounds was as memorable as Brown, but one player signed as a free agent in 1975 made a significant contribution. Eastern Michigan defensive end John Banaszak played a role in the 1975 Super Bowl run and eventually became a starter during the latter part of his seven seasons with the Steelers. He started in two Super Bowls (1978-79) and also played three seasons in the United States Football League (USFL) where he won the league title with the Michigan Panthers in 1983. The former U.S. Marine also coached in college at Washington and Jefferson and Robert Morris universities. He is the assistant head coach to Joe Walton at RMU.

"I made a very young defending Super Bowl championship team as an undrafted rookie free agent, but I was an older guy at 25," Banaszak said. "And not a whole lot of people gave me a chance to make that team. I remember the first day of training camp when George Perles told us that we could forget about beating out L.C. Greenwood, Joe Greene, Ernie Holmes, or Dwight White.

"The only way we were going to make that roster was by playing on the special teams. That's all I needed to hear, was a way to make the team. I worked hard and played pretty well on special teams in the preseason and was one of only three rookies to make that team. So, Perles was right."

Perles also told Banaszak that his role on the 1975 Steelers would be simple. He basically would be the entire scout team for the offensive and defensive lines, and his job was to get those units ready to play each week.

"He told me I could forget about playing in a game and to concentrate on getting everyone else ready to play and also to play well on the special teams," Banaszak said. "He didn't lie to me. He was right. Other than a couple of mop-up situations at the end of a game, I didn't get any serious playing time until early November against the Houston Oilers. Dwight was going to miss the game because of an ankle, [and] Steve Furness would replace him. That left me as the only available substitute defensive lineman on the sideline.

"Sure enough, in the middle of the second quarter L.C. got his leg caught in a pile and injured his leg. While the medical staff was taking care of L.C. on the field, George was pretty frantic while talking to me. He said: 'You can't get hooked, you can't get cut. Oh my God, isn't there anyone else I can put in the game?' Of course, I nodded and told him that I was the only one left. He repeated his obviously panicked words and as I was leaving the sideline, he pulled me back and said: 'Don't blow it.' With that motivational message stamped on my brain, I ran onto the field."

Banaszak realized that this was his big chance to show the Steelers, as well as the other NFL teams, that he could play in the league. He certainly didn't want to blow that opportunity and said he actually calmed down when he saw all the Pro Bowl players surrounding him in the defensive huddle. Then, it dawned on Banaszak that the Oilers probably would run right at the rookie to test him.

"They really had no success running the ball at Steve or Ernie or Joe, so they would try to run at me," Banaszak said. "Sure enough, they ran a power (running play) right at me, and we stuffed it. It was now third-and-long and an obvious passing situation. . . . I was going to use my best and only pass rush move, a bull rush, and it worked. On the first two significant plays in my NFL career, I had a solo tackle and a sack. That's not too bad.

"I was so excited that I raised both arms in the air and ran off the field, becoming the first player in the history of the NFL to celebrate a sack. What made that day more memorable, however, was that my teammates gave me the highest honor that a player can get, and that's to give him a game ball. I'll never forget how special that moment was."

The Steelers earned a second straight AFC Central Division title in 1975 with 11 straight wins and 12-2 overall record. They beat the Baltimore Colts (28-10) and Oakland Raiders (16-10) in the playoffs to set up a 21-17 victory against the Dallas Cowboys in Super Bowl X. To get ready for the playoff run and the Super Bowl, Steelers legendary radio commentator Myron Cope was charged with creating a gimmick to involve the Steelers fans, and he created the Terrible Towel. It debuted December 27, 1975. The Steelers won that game, ripped through the playoffs and the Super Bowl. The Steelers were champions for the second straight season, joining Green Bay and Miami as back-to-back Super Bowl winners. But the Steelers' torrid run was not finished. There were two non-Super Bowl seasons before they had another shot at the Lombardi Trophy, but the 1976 season had a chance to be just as super, beginning with the draft. And the Terrible Towel has been an integral part of all Steelers celebrations and the Steelers Nation's game accessories ever since.

The Steelers selected Clemson tight end Bennie Cunningham in the first round (1976-85) and added Washington offensive lineman Ray Pinney (1976-78, 80-82, 85-87) and Boston College quarterback Mike Kruczek (1976-79) in the second round. Their second pick in Round 4 was Arizona wideout Theo Bell (1976, 1978-80), and they also had two sixth-round picks—Miami, Florida, defensive tackle Gary Dunn (1976, 1978-87) and Salem (West Virginia) College running back Jack Deloplaine (1976-79). All those players contributed in some way during the 1976 season and future ones as well.

"When I was drafted by the Steelers in 1976, I was thrilled, but I also was surprised," Kruczek said. "I thought

Terry Hanratty and Joe Gilliam were the backups, so I was a little confused. I guess I really didn't know the situation at the time, but going to Pittsburgh was incredibly exciting for me. I was drafted by a team that had consecutive Super Bowl victories, great ownership, and was only four hours from where I grew up [Washington, D.C.]."

Dunn was a long way from Coral Gables, Florida, and he was a serious long shot to make the Steelers with a veteran defensive line already on the roster. But that didn't deter him from having a great attitude and a strong preseason.

"The draft was kind of weird that year, because the players' union attacked the draft, whether the NFL was allowed to do it," Dunn said. "I don't remember exactly what it was. I waited around, but nobody called. So, I went out for a few beers, and my roommates told me that the Steelers called and wanted to talk with me. So, I went back to my apartment and called them. They said they drafted me and told me when to come to Pittsburgh. I was excited, but after a while I wasn't so sure. You know, the Steelers had just won two Super Bowls, and they had a great defense with the Steel Curtain defensive line. I wondered how I would make the team, because it was a veteran team.

"And I didn't know if that was the best team for me. But I just went out and busted my butt. I worked out as hard as I could, everything I could to be in the best shape of my life and the strongest. I didn't want to get there and feel like I didn't do enough if they ended up getting rid of me. So, I ran with some guys who were linebackers and not linemen. I figured if I could hang with them, I'd be all right. And when I saw them years later, they still mention that I was in great shape after college. They said: 'No matter how much running we did, you were right behind us the entire time.' I'm very proud of that, working hard and making the Steelers. I felt like I was ready for anything."

Dunn explained that while he was somewhat intimidated by the whole situation, there were ample opportunities for rookies to make a team back then. There were six preseason games (through 1977), and the Steelers played an extra one because they won the Super Bowl. The winner of that game opened with an exhibition against a college all-star team. If Dunn lasted through training camp, which opened from 10 days to two weeks prior to that opening preseason game (so, basically, two months), he said he would have made more money than he ever had and also would have some good game tape to show to other teams.

"I didn't know how long I would last, but I gave it my best shot," Dunn recalled. "When the veterans got there, I sat up on the hill at Saint Vincent College and watched all the Mercedes and Lincolns pull into the parking lot. I had a 1970 GTO and I'm from Miami, so I just had one winter coat that I threw in the trunk in case I made the team. That's about all I had. You know, I'll never forget when Joe Greene pulled up in his Lincoln. That's a big man, but that was a big car.

"Joe got out, and kids swarmed him. He opened his trunk, and the kids reached in and pulled out shoulder pads. I wondered what the heck was going on. Does Joe Greene bring his own shoulder pads? I didn't know what to think, but one thing hasn't changed for rookies from Day 1. We had to sing in the cafeteria, carry veterans' trays, get food for them, and carry their pads and helmets on the field. But we got to work against the best players in the league during practice. That helped me make the team and get ready for the season."

The Steelers opened 1976 at Oakland and lost a tough 31-28 decision. They came back with a 31-14 win against the Cleveland Browns at home, but then they dropped three straight—to the New England Patriots at home (30-27), at

Minnesota (17-6) and at Cleveland (18-16)—and lost quarterback Terry Bradshaw in the process. Browns defensive lineman Joe "Turkey" Jones sacked Bradshaw and spiked him head first into the ground. "Jefferson Street" Joe Gilliam and Terry Hanratty, who fueled a quarterback controversy in previous years, were no longer on the team. So, the Steelers were thin at quarterback with Bradshaw incapacitated for a time.

Bradshaw's backup was Boston College All-American Kruczek, a rookie second-round pick, and he took the reins of the offense for the two-time defending Super Bowl champion Steelers. Kruczek started six straight games while Bradshaw was injured, and the Steelers won all six to improve to 7-4. He completed 60 percent of his passes (51-for-85) for 758 yards. He had no touchdowns and just three interceptions. The Steelers clearly relied heavily on their running game with Franco Harris and Rocky Bleier, and they beat Cincinnati, the New York Giants, San Diego Chargers, Kansas City Chiefs, Miami Dolphins, and Houston Oilers in succession with Kruczek at quarterback.

"The entire team did a great job making sure that I was OK, that I wasn't stressed out or anything," Kruczek. "They took a lot of the weight off my shoulders, but I gained confidence with every snap. I knew that I was playing with the best team in the NFL. [And] going 6-0 as a starter as a rookie for the Steelers was the single biggest personal accomplishment of my career.

"The coaches did a great job of simplifying things for me and making it easier for me to manage the game. Actually, it was really simple. We had to play great defense, have a solid kicking game, run the ball well, and don't turn the ball over. When you look back at those games, that's the way that we won. I didn't make too many mistakes. We ran the ball really well with Franco and Rocky and dominated on defense. Those guys were great in every game."

When Bradshaw returned, the Steelers beat the Bengals again and the Tampa Bay Buccaneers and won at Houston for nine straight wins to close the season with a 10-4 record. The Steel Curtain defense also was in high gear with five shutouts in those nine victories. It also allowed just a field goal in two games and six points in another. The only other game in the streak was a 32-16 win against the Oilers, but a late touchdown spoiled that one.

Harris finished 1976 with 1,128 rushing yards and 14 touchdowns, while Bleier added 1,036 and five scores. Reggie Harrison also contributed 235 yards and four touchdowns. With the offense running efficiently and the defense dominating, the Steelers rolled to a 40-14 win against the Baltimore Colts in the opening playoff round. However, Harris and Bleier were injured during that game, and Fuqua was battling a hamstring injury. So, Harrison was the only healthy back for the AFC championship game against Oakland. The Steelers hung tough, but the Raiders prevailed, 24-7, on their way to a Super Bowl win. Some believe this was the best Steelers team ever, although it is not officially recognized in this way. That denotation would come a couple years later, but the 1976 group would be remembered for its special season nonetheless.

A Dunn Deal

Gary Dunn was one of the true characters to play for the Steelers over the years, but he probably honed those characteristics at the University of Miami. While he didn't believe it would be easy to make the Steelers roster as a fresh-faced rookie in 1976, Dunn didn't realize how well he actually fit in.

"Our first practice with the veterans, defensive line coach George Perles told us we were going to go through a drill called head-butts," Dunn said. "And Coach, he looked at me with my last name, Dunn, scribbled on the back of my helmet, and he said: 'Hey, Dunn. You're going to set the head-butt record today.' I said: 'OK, Coach, that's great.' I thought about it years later, but those 60 head-butts we had per day at practice probably weren't a good thing in the long run. But we didn't know any better back then. Defensive linemen are supposed to be quick with their heads and hands to try to stand up an offensive lineman.

"I was playing an offensive lineman in this drill and got to L.C. Greenwood. He's a tall, lanky guy, so I thought I could get underneath him and use my strength to put him on his head. The guy who gets his helmet under the other guy, he usually wins that battle. Everybody's yelling at me: 'Watch out for the cape.' I didn't know what the heck it was, but we lined up and came off the ball. He moved to the side, and I got nothing but air. L.C. just looked at me and said: 'Hey, Rook. That's the cape.' That was my introduction to the NFL, courtesy of L.C. Greenwood. Ah, those were the days. What a great bunch of guys.

"Guys like Steve Furness and John Banaszak, they helped me out a lot. Joe Greene, L.C., Dwight White, Ernie Holmes, they were all pretty good guys. But Holmes, he scared the heck out of me. I remember the first practice with the vets, here's Holmes on the field wearing a big rubber suit. His whole body was covered. Just slits for his eyes. Well, halfway through practice, he goes down. Trainers packed him with ice to cool him down. They said he did that every year to lose weight. It was something to see."

After practice, the players worked out in the nearby gym and then had some free time. Dunn noticed that all the veteran players got in their cars and drove off for that hour or so that was available, but they all returned around the same time every day. After a few times, Dunn's curiosity got the best of him.

"I had to find out what they were doing, so I followed them," Dunn said. "I noticed that they were all parked at the 19th hole, a bar down the road, so I parked my car and went in. When I opened the door, it was like E. F. Hutton. You know, everybody stopped doing what they were doing and looked at me. They were drinking iced-down Rolling Rocks with a lime in them. That's before it was the way to drink a Corona, so those guys were way ahead of their time.

"I didn't know if it was such a good idea, but L.C. Greenwood turned around and said: 'Hey, rook, what are you doing here?' I told him I was there to have a couple beers, and he told me to come on over and have a seat. From that time on, I was part of their afternoon beer club. I also didn't realize that after drinking all the fluids during practice, you're really full. So, after a few beers, you're hungry again. So, it was real helpful to go drinking with those guys."

While Dunn got to hang out with the veterans on the defensive line, he probably learned as much about playing his position from working out with the Steelers offensive linemen, such as Larry Brown, Jon Kolb, Craig Wolfley, Tunch Ilkin, Steve Courson, Sam Davis, Gerry Mullins, and Mike Webster. Tunch and Wolf, as the pair are known today as Steelers radio announcers, have remained good friends with Dunn. During Ilkin's rookie season, he was Dunn's roommate. Dunn remembered both as being "a little off." Ilkin and Wolfley would counter that it takes one to know one. That's the type of characters the Steelers had back then. One of the biggest, literally and figuratively, was Webster. And Dunn found that out rather quickly during his rookie training camp.

"I went up against Webby every day," Dunn said. "In the four-three [defense], I was lined up on the guards, but when we changed to a three-four—maybe my fifth or sixth year in the league, 1982 or '83—they moved me to nose tackle, and I went up against Webby. Everybody knows that he was the best center in the league. One of the best ever. On Saturdays in camp, we would scrimmage. I mean, we banged heads all week in practice anyway, but on Saturday we went live. I said to Webby, 'You're an All-Pro, how about taking it easy on me.' I was friends with him at that point and thought I could ask him that, and he said: 'No problem. I'll take it easy today.' I was so glad to hear that.

"Well, on the very first play, Webby drove me back to our linebackers and threw me on Jack Lambert's feet. Lambert said: 'Hey, Dunn, if you can't play the position, get off the field.' Webby pushed me all over the field, so I was dejected when I left that day. We had the night off, so I got in my car and drove back to Pittsburgh. Well, while I was on the Pennsylvania Turnpike, here comes Webby driving past me, and he waves at me. Well, I wasn't too happy, so I shot him the bird. He made me pull over and said: 'What's wrong?' I told him that he made me look silly. 'I was terrible out there. They're gonna cut me,' I said. He said: 'No, you did good. You did good.' Then, he told me to sit down.

"He had a cooler," Dunn added. "He pulled out a couple beers from there and gave one to me, and we sat there and talked about practice. Then, he got up and showed me what I was doing wrong with my hands. Before you know it, we're doing drills right there on the side of the Pennsylvania Turnpike. After a while, he said: 'Come on, Dunny, push me back to my truck.' So, I drove him back to the truck and put him on the hood.' Then, he said: 'That was great. Let's go again.' So, we lined up and fired off. He picked me up and drove me over the guard rail. Then, he waved goodbye and said: 'Have a nice day.' So, that was my Webster experience. He was something else."

Dunn noted that he also got a good deal of help from Banaszak and Furness. They basically took him under their wings and showed him the ropes. In fact, during Dunn's rookie season, Furness was his roommate when the Steelers were on the road. There were other stories from Dunn's rookie season.

"My mom sent me a cake from a local bakery on my birthday, August 24, while we were at training camp," Dunn said. "I don't know what my mom told them, but I got this cake with a girl in a bikini on it. Picture the nuns serving this cake after lunch at the cafeteria. That one was hard to explain, but that's when we realized that I had the same birth date as Banaszak and Gerry Mullins. And every year after that, we got off a little early from practice, because Chuck knew we were going to celebrate our birthdays. So, that wasn't too bad.

"We practiced on the turf in Three Rivers Stadium during the season, but the Rooneys thought it was a good idea to practice on grass, too, since we played on grass fields occasionally during the season. So, they bought a grass area down from the stadium, and we'd dress at the stadium and walk down to this grass field in full uniform. That was a sight to see. People would drive by, honk their horns, and sometimes fans would give players a ride to the field. It was an interesting situation. After a while, some guys would get headaches from the bus fumes from the city buses driving by. Yeah, that was pretty interesting."

Dunn also conveyed a story about one of his good friends on the Steelers, massive offensive lineman Steve Courson.

"Steve was just a huge, muscle-bound guy, and he would flex his muscles like the bodybuilders would do," Dunn said. "He especially liked to do the crab pose. One time, Steve was visiting me in Coral Cables, and we were running around in my customized van with Steve in the back dancing around to the music I was playing. After a while, I saw flashing lights in my rearview mirror, and two cops pulled me over. The one stayed near the back, but the other one came to the window and asked me if I knew why he pulled me over. I said: 'No, officer. I don't think I was speeding.' He said: 'You weren't, but your van is bouncing all around and all over the place. What's in the back there?'

"I said: 'Oh, that's my friend. He's doing the crab.' Of course, neither of them knew what the crab was, so I told Steve to show them the crab. They're shining their flashlights at Steve at this point, and he says: 'Do you want to see the crab?' The first officer said yes, and then Steve asked the second one. 'Do you want to see it?' The second officer said that he did, and then Steve ripped off his shirt and flexed his muscles while doing the crab for them. They looked really stunned, and they said: 'Listen, I'd like you and it to keep driving and get out of my town. We don't even know what that was.' We got out of there pretty quick after that. Yeah, that was Steve Courson at his finest."

Dunn might have had a rough start in the NFL, but he still lasted 12 years in the league, all with the Steelers. He played just five games, but was put on injured reserve as a rookie in 1976 to open a roster spot after Terry Bradshaw was injured. Dunn also missed the 1977 season with a knee injury, but he returned in 1978 and remained a key player for the Steelers until 1987.

And the Steelers were glad to have Dunn play an integral role on their team for so long, especially since he fit so perfectly.

The Team of the Decade States its Case

The Steelers picked up eight players in 1977, including seven during the annual NFL Draft, that would be integral parts of their team during the remainder of the 1970s and into the '80s to help the franchise earn two more Super Bowl victories and become the 1970s Team of the Decade with an unprecedented four Lombardi Trophies in six years.

In the first round during the 1977 NFL Draft, the Steelers selected New Mexico linebacker Robin Cole, and he lasted from 1977-87. Northwestern State-Louisiana running back Sydney Thornton was taken in the second round (1977-82), while Michigan wideout Jimmy Smith was the second of two third-round picks (1977-82). The first of two fourth-round picks was Eastern Illinois offensive lineman Ted Peterson (1977-83, 1987), and there were three fifth-round picks. They were Youngstown State quarterback Cliff Stoudt (1977-83), South Carolina offensive guard Steve Courson (1978-83), and Arkansas linebacker Dennis "Dirt" Winston (1977-81). Minnesota quarterback Tony Dungy, who would play defensive back in the NFL, was signed as a free agent and would last two seasons with the Steelers (1977-78).

Cole noted that the Steelers had a reason for taking an outside linebacker with their No. 1 pick. Pro Bowler Andy Russell had retired, and backup Loren Toews needed some competition for the starting spot. So, they brought in Cole to have the two compete to be Russell's replacement.

"I was very excited about the opportunity to play for the Steelers after they made me their No. 1 pick," Cole said. "I got there as early as possible so I could learn their defense, and I think that put me ahead of the game a little bit. Sure, I was nervous, but it wasn't because I was unprepared. I picked things up pretty quick, and I was ready when Loren got hurt in camp. I started all the preseason games and was on a roll going into the season. But I broke my arm in the first game, and that set me back for about two months. I played with a cast on my arm the rest of the way, and it's really tough playing basically with one arm.

"When we went into the next season, I shared the position with Loren. That was frustrating, because I felt like I was ready to be a full-time starter. But that's how it goes, and we really did push each other and help each other. I believe we were the best linebacking corps in the league, and I could have led the team in sacks with my aggressive play. But I wasn't supposed to rush the passer very often. You know, we had the Steel Curtain up front. So, I just played the run strong and dropped into coverage when needed. I wasn't too heavy, so I could cover pretty far downfield. All our backers could drop into coverage."

The 1977 group helped the Steelers post a 9-5 record during the regular season, but the 1977 squad lost its opening playoff game, 34-21, against the Denver Broncos. While that might have been somewhat unexpected, the Steelers were still on the precipice of greatness. And they wouldn't have to wait too long, as the 1978 team would post the franchise's best record until rookie Ben Roethlisberger led the Steelers to a 15-1 mark in 2004. In 1978, the Steelers made history after a league-best 14-2 regular season and playoff wins against Denver (33-10) and Houston (34-5). A 35-31 Super Bowl XIII win against the Dallas Cowboys made the Steelers the first NFL franchise to win three Super Bowls. Yet another standard was set the following year when the 1979 Steelers defeated the Los Angeles Rams, 31-19, in Super Bowl XIV to make them the first team in history to win four Super Bowls and the only team to win back-to-back Super Bowls twice. The Super Bowl victory followed a 12-4 regular season and playoff wins against Miami (34-14) and Houston (27-13). With six straight AFC Central crowns, eight consecutive playoff appearances and four Super Bowls, the Steelers were tagged the "Team of the Decade" for the 1970s.

The 1978 draft played a small part in the club's Super Bowl runs, as Eastern Michigan cornerback Ron Johnson was taken in the first round and played for the Steelers from 1978-84. Tennessee punter Craig Colquitt was taken in the third round (1978-81, 83-84), while two other key players were signed as free agents. They were Virginia Tech defensive lineman Tom Beasley (1978-83) and South Carolina offensive guard Steve Courson (1978-83).

In 1979, the Steelers selected Baylor running back Greg Hawthorne with their first-round pick and added East Carolina linebacker Zack Valentine in the second round (1979-81). In the fourth round, Southern Cal wideout Calvin Sweeney was brought aboard (1980-87), while North Carolina A&T defensive end Dwaine Board was taken in the fifth round. He was cut before the season and eventually hooked up with the San Francisco 49ers where he spent nine seasons and won two Super Bowls. The Steelers also had two sixth-round picks who made an immediate impact. They were Louisville cornerback Dwayne Woodruff (1979-85, 1987-90), and Penn State place-kicker Matt Bahr (1979-80).

That wrapped the 1970s for the Steelers, who accomplished the most in any decade for any NFL team. And it certainly was a spectacular run for the league's former lovable losers. And with what they believed were solid late-decade draft picks, the Steelers were poised to continue their successful run during the 1980s. But that would be easier said than done.

Chapter 6

The 1980s

Hope Fades Fast

Considering all they had accomplished during the 1970s, the Pittsburgh Steelers believed the success would carry over into the 1980s. That assessment couldn't have been further from the truth. The 1979 NFL Draft yielded little to no talent on par with previous drafts from the decade. In fact, the Steelers didn't draft any future Hall-of-Famers until late in the 1980s. The No. 1 picks, even though many remained with the club for a half-dozen years on average, were not all-stars. Some barely made the team and didn't last long, while others didn't last at all. And this mixed bag led to disappointment more often than not for the Steelers during the 1980s, even though some believed it wasn't so bad.

"We didn't have a losing season for 12 straight years [with Chuck Noll as the head coach]," Art Rooney Jr. said. "Then, everyone said it was so bad in the 1980s, but we only had three losing seasons and went to the playoffs four times. It was nothing compared to the 1970s, to be sure, but from the '30s through the '60s there was limited success to no success. So, we were still on the plus side compared to those decades."

While Rooney Jr.'s statement is historically accurate, the bad times were seriously bad during the 1980s, including third-place finishes in 1985 (7-9), '86 (6-10) and '87 (8-7), along with a fourth-place performance and low point in 1988 (5-11). Remember, the Steelers were coming off an amazingly successful decade and then went 42-31 from 1980-84. However, they were just 9-7 in 1980 and 8-8 in 1981, and they did not make the playoffs after either season.

The Steelers believed they found the heir-apparent to Terry Bradshaw when they used the 28th overall pick in the first round during the 1980 NFL Draft to select Arizona State quarterback Mark Malone. Now an accomplished broadcaster, Malone played for the Steelers from 1980-87. However, his biggest impact was not so much as a quarterback, but as a runner and receiver. He set a franchise record with a 90-yard reception for a touchdown in 1981 and ran for 14 touchdowns during seven years with the Steelers. He completed 50.2 percent of his passes for the Steelers for 8,582 yards and 54 touchdowns with 68 interceptions. It wasn't an awful performance, but Malone didn't play at a championship level. His stay in Pittsburgh ended after the 1987 season. He played for the San Diego Chargers in 1988 and New York Jets in 1989. He played just one game for the Jets and completed only two passes, but he started eight of 12 games played for the Chargers and completed 54 percent of his passes for 1,580 yards. He had just six touchdown passes and 13 interceptions.

Rounds 2-4 produced some nice players, but none who contributed much of anything to the Steelers. They hit the jackpot in the fifth and sixth rounds, respectively, with a pair of offensive linemen in Syracuse guard Craig Wolfley and Indiana State tackle Tunch Ilkin. The two were solid performers for the Steelers, as Wolfley played for them from 1980-89 and Ilkin lasted until 1992, but their contribution to the franchise didn't stop there. The two now are part of the Steelers Radio Network. Ilkin is a color commentator with play-by-play man Bill Hillgrove, while Wolfley is the sideline reporter.

In the 11th round, the Steelers picked up another Baylor running back in stocky fullback Frank Pollard, who played for them from 1980-88. And selection 12b, known as Mr. Irrelevant due to being the final pick in the entire draft, was Florida A&M offensive guard Tyrone McGriff. He stayed with the Steelers for three seasons (1980-82) before hooking up with the USFL's Michigan Panthers.

GREAT EXPECTATIONS

The Steelers had the 17th overall pick in the first round during the 1981 NFL Draft and picked Oklahoma defensive end Keith Gary, who played for the club from 1983-88 after a couple seasons in Canada. The Steelers didn't hit on another selection until their sixth- and seventh-round choices—Oregon outside linebacker Bryan Hinkle (1982-93) and Miami, Fla. inside linebacker David Little (1981-92), respectively—and that was about it for 1981.

In 1982, the Steelers had an even higher pick. With the 12th overall selection in the first round during the draft that year, they picked Baylor running back Walter Abercrombie (1982-87). Abercrombie basically was selected to be the heir-apparent to future Hall-of-Fame running back Franco Harris, who was nearing the end of his spectacular career. Abercrombie played 21 games during his opening two seasons, ran for 546 yards and six touchdowns and added 27 catches for 405 yards and another three scores, while Harris was still the lead back. In the strike-shortened 1982 season, Harris played nine games and ran for 604 yards and two touchdowns; he played the entire 1983 season and ran for 1,007 yards and five scores. He also had 65 catches for 527 yards and two touchdowns combined in 1982-83.

"You could look at my career a couple different ways," Abercrombie said. "If you look at it in terms of an evaluation, I'd say that I was probably . . . I had great potential, and the Steelers expected great things from me. And it was an unbelievable challenge, basically, to take up where a future Hall-of-Famer left off. But filling his shoes was an impossible task. Franco was still on the team when I got there, and the first couple years that I played with Franco I didn't feel as much pressure because he was still there.

"It was after he left that an amazing weight was placed on me. If you recall, the Steelers could not come to an agreement with Franco on his contract, and he eventually signed with Seattle before the 1984 season. [But] I had every reason to believe that the Steelers were going to sign him, because why would you take a chance on losing a legend like that? So, mentally, I just wasn't ready to assume that duty, to be that guy in the offense. I guess, in retrospect, I should have always been ready to be the guy, but hindsight is always 20-20."

There are some who believe that Abercrombie never was ready to be the man for the Steelers, but that doesn't mean he didn't have a few successful seasons. And it doesn't mean that the 1982 NFL Draft was poor. Sure, the No. 2 pick didn't pan out, but the Steelers got talented linebacker Mike Merriweather from Pacific in the third round. And he lasted from 1982-87. Auburn defensive tackle Edmund Nelson (1982-87) came to the Steelers through their first pick in the seventh round, and he has remained connected to the team. He does some broadcasting work and makes certain that each player's uniform is in compliance with league standards. Two other key players—place-kicker Gary Anderson from Syracuse (1982-94) and defensive end Keith Willis from Northeastern (1982-87, 1989-91)—were signed. Hinkle did not play in 1981, so his lengthy Steelers career began in 1982. Willis was injured in '88.

However, as their No. 1 pick and 12th overall selection, Abercrombie was the key to the 1982 NFL Draft for the Steelers. In the nine games during the strike-shortened 1982 season—which was also the franchise's 50th anniversary season—the Steelers were 6-3. The club made the playoffs, but lost, 31-28, to San Diego. Unfortunately for the Steelers, this was the last playoff game at Three Rivers Stadium for a decade (until the 1992 season). Abercrombie ran for 100 yards and two touchdowns on 21 carries in six games as a rookie, while Harris led the Steelers with 604 yards and two touchdowns. He added 31 catches for 249 yards and no scores. Abercrombie's former Baylor teammate, Pollard, was second on the team in rushing with 238 yards and two scores. Another Baylor back, Greg Hawthorne, had 68 yards rushing to go with 12 catches for 182 yards and three scores. Sidney Thornton and Russell Davis were the other Steelers running backs that season. Hawthorne primarily was used as a receiver later in his career, and he had just one carry during his final four NFL seasons with the New England Patriots (1984-86) and Indianapolis Colts (1987). Abercrombie's contribution to the offense eventually changed as well.

"As far as the Steelers offense went, I think I probably was more suited to a different style," Abercrombie said. "They liked to run traps and things like that, mostly in between the tackles, while I'm better suited to running sweeps and things like that. Running more outside than inside. Marcus Allen and I were very similar types of backs. He went to an offense that probably was better suited for me. Marcus benefited from the style of offense that he played in, and the Steelers style was better suited for Franco than it was for me. Franco was a bigger back, and the same could be said about Pollard and Thornton. But one thing about the Steelers is that later in my career, Tom Moore, our offensive coordinator, found out that I could catch the ball.

"So, I had a lot more success as a third-down back coming out of the backfield to catch passes. I could stay on the field for every down, which saved my career. So, I was able to play a few more years. We had Louis Lipps on the outside, and Stallworth was still there. So, we had some good players to throw the ball to down the field, but I was another option out of the backfield. We had some young receivers in the mix, too, but we really never threw the ball to the backs until Tom Moore got there. There were some big linebackers in the league during that time, and they had trouble covering me down the field. So, that was a little wrinkle in our offense that Tom Moore, to his credit, put in that made us a little different from what Steelers fans were used to seeing."

Harris wasn't the only future Hall-of-Famer in the final years of his Steelers career. The club's 1982 roster also included quarterback Terry Bradshaw, cornerback Mel Blount, offensive tackle Larry Brown, outside linebacker Jack Ham, middle linebacker Jack Lambert, safety Donnie Shell, wideouts John Stallworth and Lynn Swann, and center Mike Webster. Mean Joe Greene and L.C. Greenwood retired after the 1981 season.

Each owned four Super Bowl rings and also had an heir apparent to replace him upon retirement, though not all of the replacements panned out for the Steelers.

"So, Franco leaves [in 1984], and all of a sudden there's a hole in the Steelers offense," Abercrombie said. "And the Steelers were struggling to figure out how I fit into their system. They knew I wasn't a big back like Franco, but I wasn't small. I played at about 210 pounds. But I was completely different from Franco. I came from a completely different system, and we struggled a little bit.

"We had a couple good years, but we also struggled as the Steelers transitioned from all those great players from the 1970s, basically, as the future Hall-of-Famers from the 1970s teams retired. The main issue, as I saw it, was that the team just wasn't prepared to handle the exodus of all those great players. It tried to bring in guys to replace them, but as they found out it's impossible to replace future Hall-of-Famers, as the old guard basically hung it up."

Many of those veterans helped with the transition as much as possible for the rookies, even though they knew that their roster spots were less secure every year. Abercrombie noted that Harris wasted no time helping him assimilate.

"Franco was a quiet guy, but a very classy guy," Abercrombie remembered. "He showed that right away. They do picture day on the first day of training camp in Latrobe [in 1982], but my agent was still working on my contract until that day. So, I didn't fly into Pittsburgh until that first day of camp. I got there and just inked my deal. They were getting ready to start camp, and there were rumors about me going to Canada, like Keith Gary, who had the same agent as me. The veterans already were on the field and taking photos, so they were ready to introduce the rookies, one at a time. They started with the last one, the 12th rounder, and went backward to get to me at No. 1.

"Finally, they get to me, and after they introduced me I ran across the field. I remember all the fans on the hillsides cheering for me, and this was my first day with the team. I had never met Franco before, but he broke out of the pack of veterans and started jogging toward me. So, we were running at each other, and I'm saying to myself: 'That's No. 32, Franco Harris.' I wondered what he thought about me. Maybe he didn't like me, because I had read that I was supposed to replace him. So, I didn't know what to think, but the fans are cheering louder and louder as we're getting closer and closer together.

"And when we finally got to midfield, Franco had a big smile on his face," Abercrombie added. "He grabbed me, pulled me close, hugged me and then whispered in my ear, 'Walter, welcome to the team.' I'm thinking to myself, 'Franco just welcomed me to the Steelers.' That was something. It meant so much to me. We jogged hand-in-hand across the field, and everybody was cheering so loud. It was amazing. It showed me right then what kind of guy he was, a future Hall-of-Famer, that he was bigger than all the rumors or anything. I'm sure he knew why the Steelers drafted a running back so high, with him near the end of his career, and he was bigger than that. What a special guy."

Harris and Abercrombie were teammates for just two seasons, because after a decade of winning—including four Super Bowls and lots of thrills for Steelers fans—the club and the future Hall-of-Famer disagreed on his new contract. This dispute led to a bitter breakup, with Harris leaving for the Seattle Seahawks. Although the sides have basically made up since then, at the time it was clear that Harris had been forced out after the 1983 season. Harris played just one sorry season in Seattle and added little to his legacy with 68 rushes for 170 yards and no touchdowns. He also had one catch for three yards in his eight games played. Over his 13-season career, Harris rushed for 12,120 yards (averaging 4.1 yards per carry) and 91 touchdowns. He also had 307 catches for nine more scores. Abercrombie had an insurmountable task to fill that void on offense in the Steelers lineup.

The 1983 NFL Draft was largely forgettable for the Steelers, and so were players such as Kansas wideout Wayne Capers, San Diego State linebacker Todd Seabaugh, and Baylor defensive back Bo Scott Metcalf—the team's picks in the second, third, and fourth rounds, respectively—but they appeared to get a special player at No. 1 with Texas Tech defensive lineman Gabe Rivera. (It's worth noting that future Hall-of-Fame quarterback and local boy Dan Marino was available, but the Steelers passed on him—along with many other teams.) Known as Señor Sack, Rivera appeared to be the dominant D-lineman the Steelers craved since members of the Steel Curtain hung it up.

"Gabe was a heckuva player," Abercrombie said. "But his career came to a tragic end, and the Steelers were set back once again. The 1984 season was pretty good, because we reached the AFC championship, but that's as close as we would get to the Super Bowl."

Rivera played in just six games and recorded two sacks, but he was coming on strong as the season neared its midpoint. The Steelers' hopes and Rivera's NFL career came crashing down on October 20, 1983, during a head-on collision. Rivera was charged with drunken driving, speeding, reckless driving, and driving on the wrong side of the road. Those charges paled in comparison to the effect on Rivera; a spinal-cord injury left him as a paraplegic.

With Swann in retirement, the lone receiving threat was Stallworth. So, the Steelers selected Southern Mississippi wideout Louis Lipps with their No. 1 pick in 1984 to pair with him. This was an excellent pick for the Steelers, as Lipps gave the club a deep threat and also a dangerous punt-returner. Other key acquisitions in 1984 included fourth-round draft picks Weegie Thompson and Terry Long and ninth-round selection Rich Erenberg from Colgate. Thompson was a wideout who played for the Steelers from 1984-89, while running back Erenberg lasted three seasons (1984-86). And Long solidified the offensive line from his guard spot from 1984-91 before emotional problems ended his career and his life. He committed suicide by drinking antifreeze in 2005. It was his second attempt to end his troubled life.

The Steelers won the AFC Central Division title in 1983 (10-6) and '84 (9-7), their eighth and ninth division titles. However, they were hammered by the then Los Angeles (not Oakland) Raiders in the 1983 playoffs. In 1984, the Steelers advanced to the AFC championship game with a stunning 24-17 playoff win at Denver. However, with a shot at a fifth Super Bowl on the line, the Steelers were humbled, 45-28, by second-year quarterback Dan Marino and the Miami Dolphins after a close first half. Abercrombie ran for 610 yards in 1984 and more than 800 in '85, but his best season was 1986 when he tallied nearly 1,300 total yards. Abercrombie ran for 877 yards and six touchdowns and added 47 catches for 395 yards and two more scores. Injuries limited him to 12 games in 1987, and that would be his final season with the Steelers.

"Back to evaluating my career," Abercrombie said, despite not being asked to grade it. "I guess I'd give myself a C. I don't know if I'd make a B. Maybe a C+, but when put in terms of the experience that I had in Pittsburgh, it was top rate. Everybody in the organization treated me well. The Rooney family, which I still believe should be considered as royalty in the NFL, they seem to have done it right all these years. From the Rooneys to all our coaches and my teammates, it was a first-class operation. I even got to know the Chief. He was in his final years, but he was a great man. I grew to admire him very much.

"I don't want to create the impression that I thought I was a bust, but I think the Steelers expected more. I wanted to achieve more, and being a first-round pick there was a tremendous amount of pressure that goes along with that anyway. And I think we struggled as a team with that. Losing Bradshaw and not really having an answer for that. Malone wasn't the answer. He had some bad knees, so he was not as mobile as he could have been. He was restricted a little bit that way, so that was an even greater challenge than I had. I think we were trying to find our way as a team. [But] I went to a team that had a number of older men on the team, many who were married and had families, so there was a tremendous amount of experience and leadership on that team.

"So, we didn't have a whole lot of discipline problems, and I didn't even try to get out of line in the least," Abercrombie added. "I didn't get up there and go buck wild or go crazy, because we had such an older and mature team. I grew up while I was in Pittsburgh. That's for sure. And with such a tremendous coach like Chuck, I was able to grow in that system. So, for me personally, it was a great experience. And playing in a city like Pittsburgh, it was fantastic. I grew up down the street from the Dallas Cowboys, and I always believed that Cowboys fans were second to none. At least that's what I thought, until I got to Pittsburgh and saw the commitment, dedication, and loyalty of those fans. So, as a player, I would just consider myself lucky to play with Hall-of-Famers, in a city that won four Super Bowls and play for a family like the Rooney family."

Abercrombie quickly realized that he didn't know how well he had it in Pittsburgh until he went to the Philadelphia Eagles in 1988. He said he got a two-year contract with the Eagles, but he played just five games and ran the ball five times for 14 yards in 1988, which was his final NFL season.

"When I went to Philadelphia, I was one of the oldest guys on the team," Abercrombie said. "And Buddy Ryan, the head coach, he called me into his office. Reggie White, Randall Cunningham, Cris Carter, Keith Jackson, they were all kids on that team. So, Buddy called me into his office with Mike Quick and Al Harris and told us that this team could be good with some leadership. He knew we were at the end of our careers, but he wanted us to be leaders and to give our experience to those talented young players. So, that's what we did.

"I look at the '80s this way with the Steelers. We played well. We won games. We won our division a couple times, and we made the playoffs. We didn't go very deep, but we had a good showing more often than not, I think, with an aging team and a team that was being rebuilt. So, if you judge that on face value, you should say that we did OK. But if you compare it to the 1970s, then we underperformed. So, I guess it all depends how you want to look at it."

Abercrombie resides in his native Texas, which makes it difficult to stay in touch with some of his ex-teammates. But that doesn't include ex-roommate Craig Bingham, a linebacker in Abercrombie's draft class. Bingham played for the Steelers from 1982 to 1984, moved on to the San Diego Chargers in 1985, but returned to the Steelers in 1987. Abercrombie and his wife, Kim, live in the Dallas area with their two sons—the "biggest

Steelers fans in Cowboys country"—Weslye, 19; and Warren, 16. Weslye is a freshman linebacker at the University of Mary Hardin-Baylor (UMHB) in Belton, Texas. His team lost to eventual Division III champion Mount Union in the semifinals in 2013. They also have two girls, Ryann, 13; and Peyton, 5. The Abercrombies married in 1992.

"I went to the Steelers-Cowboys game this past year in Dallas [2012], and when we got to the parking lot I was just so surprised," Abercrombie said. "You would not believe the number of Steelers fans who were there for the game. You could see all the different jerseys, Ben, Polamalu, a bunch of Hines Ward, a lot of them. It was almost like the Steelers had a home game.

"Steelers fans were everywhere. And the fans always treated me good. I had an injury my rookie season, and I struggled a little bit with my knee. Once we got rolling, I felt like the fans were fair to me, but it was tough for them. They were so used to winning, those great, dominant teams, and through the early parts of the '80s and '90s we were not the same Steelers of old. So, the fans were dealing with that a little bit, and they might have reacted accordingly.

"It seems like the Steelers are rebuilding now," Abercrombie added. "I'm sure they don't like that term, but when you go 8-8 and miss the playoffs, then you have to dump some guys and will lose a few more, that must be termed as rebuilding. I still try to keep up with the Steelers, but I probably follow college football a little more than the NFL since I'm involved with athletics here at Baylor. So, I keep an eye on my Steelers, but that's about it for the NFL. I came back a few years ago, brought my kids for the oldest one's 16th birthday, went to a game, got introduced to the crowd [during the 75th season celebration]. It was cool."

Abercrombie is an associate athletic director at Baylor, working as executive director of the "B" Association, which basically is the Baylor Lettermen's Club. It's a 4,000-member group that Abercrombie has helmed since 2004. And he still cheers for the Steelers every chance he gets. It was especially difficult to be a Steelers fan during the latter half of the 1980s. The Steelers' streak of 13 consecutive non-losing seasons ended in 1985 with a 7-9 finish, and they followed that with a 6-10 mark in 1986. Playoff hopes remained alive in 1987 until the Steelers lost their last two games to finish 8-7 during a season shortened by one game due to a strike.

That moderate success was fleeting, however, as the 1988 Steelers stumbled through their worst season in two decades to finish at 5-11. The decade of the 1980s appeared to be on its way to ending with a whimper for the Steelers, as the 1989 season began with humiliating losses to the Cleveland Browns (51-0) and Cincinnati Bengals (41-10). And the offense failed to score during the first month that season. Things turned around for the Steelers, and they finished at 9-7 in 1989 to earn a wild-card playoff berth after a win in the regular-season finale. In the playoffs, Gary Anderson kicked a field goal in overtime to win at Houston, 24-23, but the season ended with a heartbreaking 26-23 loss at Denver. The Steelers led that divisional playoff game until the waning minutes.

There are several reasons why the Steelers fell on hard times for a few years, but the main one is failures in the NFL Draft. In 1985, with the 20th overall pick, they selected Wisconsin defensive end Darryl Sims. He lasted just two seasons (1985-86), while second-round pick Mark Behning—an offensive tackle from Nebraska—didn't play in 1985 and left the club after the 1986 season. The only pick who made an impact, ironically, was eighth-rounder Harry Newsome. The punter from Wake Forest played for the Steelers from 1985-89.

The 1986 draft yielded three top choices who were with the Steelers for an extended period. Temple offensive guard John Rienstra (1986-90) was the No. 1 pick, followed by Auburn defensive tackle Gerald Williams (1986-94) and Louisiana-Monroe quarterback Bubby Brister (1986-92) in the second and third rounds, respectively. The next two drafts finally secured two Hall-of-Famers for the Steelers. Purdue cornerback Rod Woodson was the Steelers No. 1 pick in 1987, 10th overall, and he excelled for the club from 1987-96. And in 1988, the second-rounder was Kentucky center Dermontti Dawson. He anchored the Steelers' offensive line from 1988-2000. Woodson was inducted into the Pro Football Hall of Fame in 2009, while Dawson finally made it in 2012.

The 1987 draft actually was packed with good players picked after Woodson. That group included Clemson cornerback "Beltin'" Delton Hall in the second round (1987-91), Baylor safety Thomas Everett in the fourth round (1987-91) and California linebacker Hardy Nickerson in the fifth round (1987-92). The two sixth-round picks were Penn State defensive tackle Tim Johnson (1987-89) and Fort Valley State outside linebacker Greg Lloyd (1988-97), while Idaho State running back Merril Hoge was taken in the 10th round (1987-93).

In 1988, with the 18th overall pick, the Steelers selected Eastern Kentucky defensive end Aaron Jones (1988-92). After Dawson in the second round, the only other decent draft pick was Miami, Florida, running back Warren Williams in the sixth round (1988-92). The Steelers also signed Eastern Kentucky offensive tackle John Jackson, and he played for the club from 1988-97.

The Search Continued

With Abercrombie gone for a couple seasons and Hoge plodding along in his third season, the Steelers still believed they needed a featured back like they had for more than a decade with Harris. That's why they used the seventh overall pick in the first round during the 1989 NFL Draft to take Georgia running back Tim Worley with the first of two opening-round selections. Later in the first round, they brought in Pitt offensive guard Tom Ricketts. Five other draft picks made an impact for the Steelers, even if it was for just a few years, but Worley was the key to this draft, as far as the franchise was concerned.

"I held out my rookie year, but it was only for a couple of weeks, before I got to my first training camp with the Steelers and Chuck Noll," Worley said. "I always kept myself in pretty good shape, physically, but I was behind when I got to camp. And I really wasn't prepared for what I would face in the NFL. It was a different level from what I was used to. And it was more different from what it was going from high school to college. The NFL is another level. It's one thing to be in good physical condition, but it's another thing to be in football shape.

"You can run all day long, but when you put pads on and have to learn the team's plays . . . those are the areas where I was behind. I needed to develop a new mind-set as well, because everybody is good in the NFL. In college, there's a big jump, of course, but it's nothing like it is from college to the pros. That's a hard thing to get in your mind, you know, that the linebackers can run just as fast as the running backs. And they're bigger, too, so you have to bring everything you've got mentally and physically every single day of the week."

Worley had a solid rookie season with 770 yards rushing and five touchdowns, but that was his best season. He ran for only 418 yards in 11 games during his second year, but injuries and a partying lifestyle curtailed the 1990-91 seasons. During the 1989 NFL Draft, the Steelers also selected UCLA safety Carnell Lake (1989-98) in the second round, Purdue outside linebacker Jerrol Williams (1989-92) in the fourth round, Kentucky cornerback David Johnson (1989-93) in the seventh round, Pitt inside linebacker Jerry Olsavsky (1989-97) in the 10th round, and Pitt-Johnstown offensive guard Carlton Haselrig (1990-93) in the 12th round. Lake and Olsavsky are assistant coaches with the Steelers. Lake is the club's secondary coach, while Olsavsky is a defensive assistant who works with the Steelers linebackers.

"My rookie year, about the fourth or fifth game, things started to click for me, and I ended up with a pretty good season," Worley said. "They started giving me the ball more, and I performed much better on the football field. I was learning the game, learning the plays, but the off-field things took hold of me. You know, I had a house in Pittsburgh. I was a single man, living on my own, not in the dorms or an apartment with teammates like I was in college. It became easy for me to make these poor choices that were available to me. Drinking, drugs, chasing women, and there were a lot of women. I had a partying habit. That all came very easy for me, and it certainly became a hindrance.

"It stopped, eventually, and that year that I was suspended really was an eye-opener for me. The 1992 season was a wake-up call for me. It actually pushed me to the point where I worked harder and became more focused, and it also showed me how much the Steelers believed in me. You know, when you get suspended for a year like that, I'm sure there are some teams that would just cut you loose. But not the Steelers. They brought me back and gave me an opportunity to make the team in 1993, even with a new coach, Bill Cowher."

Worley played just two games and ran for 117 yards on 22 carries in 1991. He was suspended on October 30, 1991, for six games for violating the NFL's drug policy after a trace of cocaine was found in his system. Since the first violation is not announced, this was his second violation. Worley immediately was placed on the Steelers' non-football illness list and was not available to play or practice until December 9. Even though Worley played the final two games, he wasn't out of the woods just yet. This is when Worley's career took an abrupt turn. He didn't show up for a mandatory drug test and was suspended by the league for the entire 1992 season. "They didn't mess around," Worley said.

It probably would be difficult to find anyone who feels bad for Worley, but he does not appear to feel sorry for himself, either. Worley confirmed that he was once a passive person, but he is assertive, now, as a motivational speaker for the company he and his wife started. Dee Worley handles leadership consulting for Worley Global Enterprises. The Worleys work with businesses, churches, formal events, sporting events, youth and NCAA programs that need guidance and leadership. They have custom-designed programs specifically tailored to each audience, group or individual. Tim also works with the Boys and Girls Clubs of North Alabama, as a mental coordinator in the corporate office in Huntsville, Ala. But it took Worley a long time to become the man that he is today.

"That year suspension woke me up, and I realized I was dealing with something that began to take control," Worley said. "It wasn't just the fact that the drugs were there and I was getting high, but it surrounded a lot of things and sort of helped me look deeper into things as I got older, like all the insecurities that I had about myself since I was a young man . . . and that I was a very passive person for a long time. A lot of things came out, all the anger and rage. There were a lot of things that I should have confronted as a young man, and I never did it. [But] I've been alcohol-free and drug-free for a lot of years now.

"As I lost everything, because of my choices, I don't have anything from my time in the NFL. I also lost two brothers, my oldest and my youngest brother—at 40 and 34—[and] I had to go back home and live with my parents. I was embarrassed and broke, busted and disgusted, and I hated myself. They'll put you up, but as soon as you get down they'll talk about you. When the money runs out, so do your friends, your so-called friends. But I don't point a finger, and I don't blame anybody. I look in the mirror and take full responsibility for everything. When you're young, you crave that attention from the ladies, and they were coming at me from the left and the right.

"But that's also the first time in my life when I didn't say no," Worley added. "I really got caught up in it all. It was very overwhelming, and I fell for it. And when I wanted to let go, I really couldn't. And by the time I wanted to let go, I found out that I had a habit. Later on in my career, right before that one-year suspension, every time I went out there was alcohol and a line of coke or a joint to smoke. That really wasn't me, and I know it wasn't me. But I was following the lead, instead of being a leader, and that wasn't good for me and my life, let alone my football career. It just wasn't good at all."

Worley described himself as a country boy from North Carolina, raised in a Christian home by parents who are still alive today. His only diversion was sports. Worley didn't drink or do drugs. He just wanted to play sports and excel at them enough to be successful in high school and eventually go to college.

"I competed in all the sports to see where they would take me, but never in my wildest dreams did I think I would be playing for my favorite team in the NFL since I was a little boy," Worley said. "I've always been a Steelers fan, since I was about 7 or 8 years old, and I was their No. 1 draft pick in 1989. That was a dream come true, but nobody tells you about all the things that come with being a No. 1 draft pick in the NFL, with having notoriety, a superstar athlete. Nobody tells you, so I had to find out about it by myself. I guess it was a mystery, what you had to do to go from high school to college to the NFL. Now, you get to see it all. There's no mystery anymore.

"With the Internet, an athlete's entire life is on display, and all the games are televised. I knew what I was capable of, and when I walked away from the game in 1996, when I officially retired, I looked back at my career. And there were a lot of things that I regretted, because I knew, I knew, deep down in my heart, that I did not put into the NFL 100 percent of myself like I did in college and like I did in high school. And I knew that, being the type of player that I was, that I could play with anybody on any given Sunday. But it was more than just the physical part of the game.

"It was also the responsibility that came with how you handled yourself off the field," Worley added. "And when I look back on it, during that season in my life, I was very immature. It was like a big party, and I looked at it like I probably was more concerned about what was going on off the field more than what went on while I was on the field. I was making good money, but I really didn't get a handle on the idea that it was a job. You have to treat it like a job, and I really didn't do that. You think the money and the life will last forever, but that's the farthest thing from the truth. So, the idea that this was a job and I needed to respect that aspect of it, that became secondary to me."

There are those who believe there was bitterness or animosity between Worley and the Steelers' new head coach, Bill Cowher, who replaced legend Chuck Noll in 1992. But Worley said that just wasn't the case. Cowher and the Steelers brought him back for the 1993 season, after his year suspension, and Worley ran for 33 yards on 10 carries in just five games before asking for a trade.

"I think the deadline was in October for a trade, and I asked them to shop me around to see if there were any teams out there who needed a running back to come right in and play," Worley said. "And Coach Cowher did that for me, because he saw my frustration, too. So, that's how I ended up with the Bears and head coach Dave Wannstedt. The Packers, Cardinals, Buccaneers, and Bears were the teams that were interested in me, and I ended up with the Bears. Coach Wannstedt knew about me in college, through some of the coaches that I was acquainted with and played for, and when he saw that I was on the trading block he went after me. And I really loved the City of Chicago.

"So, I really appreciated what Coach Cowher did to facilitate my move to Chicago. He was the type of guy where you could go into his office and talk to him. You know, I've had some great coaches in my life. My high school coach, Ruffin McNeill, he's the head coach at East Carolina right now. He coached me in football, basketball, and track. Then, I went to Georgia, and Hall-of-Famer Vince Dooley was the head coach [from 1964-88 and AD from 1979-2004]. Then, I got drafted by the Steelers and played for Hall-of-Fame coach Chuck Noll. Bill Cowher, who I think eventually will be in the Hall of Fame, took over for Chuck. And then I played for Dave Wannstedt in Chicago."

Worley played 10 games for the Bears in 1993 and ran for 437 yards and two touchdowns. He added 17 yards and one score on nine attempts during his final NFL season in 1994. So, Worley never matched the offensive output he had as an NFL rookie with the Steelers in 1989. Sure, Noll might have recognized Worley's talent and challenged him to be a better player that year, as well as a better person, but he still tried to stick the square peg player in a round hole in his offense. The Steelers generally were a trapping team with their backs primarily running between the tackles. That wasn't Worley's forte, as he rarely blocked in college and usually ran pitch plays out of the I-formation.

"They put me in a three-point stance with the Steelers, who usually ran a lot of traps, and I was doing a lot of blocking as well," Worley said. "That was a challenge in itself for me. Chuck knew I had the skills and ability to adjust and do what I wanted on the field, so he believed in me. But he also saw the other side, the heavy-duty responsibilities from being a high No. 1 pick weighing on my shoulders. And he saw that I was starting to crumble. So, it was very heavy, but that was a season in my life where I didn't realize my identity.

"I thought I was just a football player, and I didn't worry about anything else. Off the field, I did whatever I wanted to do in order to have a good time. So, I was very immature, and I hit a lot of sabotage buttons. Every time things went well, I hit those buttons and sabotaged everything. I was never one of these cats who would just drink and get high every day. It was just sporadic for me, but to be honest with you it was all about the girls. Going out and chasing the girls, having a good time, that's what I was all about off the field."

It's been quite a while since Worley has been back in Pittsburgh, but he planned a visit in 2013 to "play in some golf tournaments," including one by Greg Lloyd.

"Greg invited me to come back, and I'm going to try to make it happen," Worley said. "Like I've said, I'm in a much better place now, certainly much better than I was during my playing days in Pittsburgh."

The Steelers organization had undergone a number of changes during the 1980s. But when Tim Worley left the team in 1993, one thing hadn't changed: the Pittsburgh Steelers were still searching for that featured running back to replace Franco Harris.

Chapter 7

The 1990s

Reigning Emperor About to Change

The Pittsburgh Steelers placed second in the AFC Central Division in 1989 with a 9-7 record, but a stunning overtime playoff win at Houston and near miss at Denver the following week, where the Steelers led until the waning minutes, buoyed hope for the next decade. However, as head coach Chuck Noll's tenure chugged into a third decade, the Steelers' fortunes changed.

The club was 9-7 again in 1990, but the Steelers officially finished third in the AFC Central after a blowout loss at Houston in the season finale forged a three-way tie for the division crown. The Steelers didn't make the grade with a 2-4 mark in divisional play, and that kept them out of the playoffs. The Cincinnati Bengals won the AFC Central, while the Oilers were second after beating the Steelers in the Astrodome in the season finale. The Cleveland Browns limped to a fourth-place finish at 3-13, but their season-opening 13-3 home win was debilitating to the Steelers, who had to finish strong after a 1-4 start.

That late-season success didn't carry over into the 1991 campaign, as the Steelers went 2-2 before the bye week and never got on a roll. They won the first game after the break, 21-3, against the Indianapolis Colts, but then dropped four straight and were 2-7 in that late-season stretch to go to 5-9 with two games remaining. The Steelers could not reach a .500 record, but at least finished at 7-9 with two home wins to end the season. They beat the Bengals and Browns each by a 17-10 score, but elation turned to sadness when Noll announced his retirement on December 26, 1991. The "Emperor" had been associated with professional football for 39 consecutive years as a player and coach, including the final 23 as the Steelers' head coach, before he abdicated his throne. When Noll retired, he had the fifth-best record in NFL history at 209-156-1, and the club's four Super Bowl wins were unprecedented for one head coach. Noll rarely received accolades during his tenure, but he was awarded the ultimate honor with induction into the Pro Football Hall of Fame in his first year of eligibility in 1993.

"I'm not sure why he never was recognized for being a great coach," Steelers tight end, offensive tackle and four-time Super Bowl champion Larry Brown said. "He was a great coach. He put together an incredible group of men who worked very well together. Sure, we had some great players on those teams in the 1970s, but there have been other teams with a lot of talent that didn't succeed like us. Chuck Noll was responsible for getting us to work together."

The Steelers got just a little help from the draft, but there were no dominant players taken during Noll's final two seasons. And any success by a player from those drafts was short-term. They had two first-round picks in 1990 and traded the first one to Dallas. With the second selection in the first round, the Steelers took tight end Eric Green from Liberty University in

Lynchburg, Virginia. Green spent five of his 10 NFL seasons (1990-94) with the Steelers and quickly was recognized as an offensive weapon. At about 6-foot-5 and 280 pounds, Green was a huge target, but also was fast and athletic. During his time with the Steelers, he tallied 198 catches for 2,681 yards (13.54 per catch) and 24 touchdowns. His best season was 1993 when he started all 16 games and had 63 catches for 942 yards and five scores. However, drug and conditioning issues dogged his Steelers tenure, and he was suspended twice for violating the league's drug policy. Green played for the Miami Dolphins in 1995, spent three seasons in Baltimore, and ended his career with the New York Jets in 1999. Green's career stats included 362 catches for 4,390 yards (12.1) and 36 touchdowns, but it is believed that he could have done much more had cocaine not been a factor for a period of time in his life.

The Steelers' second-round pick was LSU defensive end Kenny Davidson, and he played for the Steelers from 1990-93. And after four forgettable seasons, when the big man tallied just eight sacks, Davidson moved on to the Houston Oilers for two seasons and ended his career with the Cincinnati Bengals in 1996. He actually had six sacks in 1994, his first season in Houston, but barely played with the Bengals and finished with 16 career sacks.

With the first of two third-round picks, the Steelers selected Maryland quarterback Neil O'Donnell (1990-95), and they picked up Arkansas running back Barry Foster (1990-94) in the fifth round. Each made an impact during his sometimes stormy tenure with the Steelers, and each left Pittsburgh on a sour note. O'Donnell eventually became the club's starting quarterback and helped them get into the Super Bowl after the 1995 season, but he threw three interceptions in a 27-17 loss to the Dallas Cowboys and left town as a goat. O'Donnell's agent, Leigh Steinberg, told reporters sometime later that O'Donnell believed he would never be viewed positively by Steelers fans after his performance in the Super Bowl. He played two solid seasons for the New York Jets (1996-97), one season in Cincinnati and ended his career with five largely forgettable seasons with the Tennessee Titans (1999-2003).

Foster's five seasons with the Steelers were the only ones he spent in the NFL, and he finished with 3,943 rushing yards, 23 touchdowns, a 4.3 average, 93 catches for 804 yards (8.6) and two more scores. But his bad attitude and poor work ethic never endeared him to Steelers fans or the club's coaches. Foster's best season was 1992 when he set a Steelers record with 1,690 yards rushing (4.3 average), 11 touchdowns, and 36 catches for 344 yards (9.6).

In the 11th round in 1990, the Steelers were fortunate to select Maine offensive lineman Justin Strzelczyk. He played 10 seasons for the Steelers (1990-99) and was a starter for 75 of the 133 games he played. While he was a member of the Steelers, Strzelczyk did not play during the 1999 season due to an injury. The 6-foot-6, 305-pound mountain man with a thick beard and jovial personality died tragically at age 36 in a car accident after a 37-mile high-speed chase with state police on Interstate 90 in New York. While the cops never caught up to him, Strzelczyk's emotional problems finally did.

Noll's final draft, in 1991, was largely forgettable. Florida outside linebacker Huey Richardson was the Steelers' first-round pick, the 15th overall selection, but he never panned out. Richardson played just five games in 1991 with the Steelers and had a two-year career that also included four games with the Washington Redskins and seven with the New York Jets in 1992. That's 16 total games with no viable statistics, and that stats line left a lot of heads shaking.

The Steelers picked up a pair of receivers in the second and third round, respectively, with Ohio State's Jeff Graham (1991-93) and Florida's Ernie Mills (1991-96). Another offensive player, Oklahoma tight end Adrian Cooper (1991-93), was taken late in the fourth round. And in the sixth round, Penn State running back Leroy Thompson (1991-93) came on board. Each lasted for several seasons, but neither was more than a marginal player.

Three Teams, 16 Games, Two Seasons, and No Stats

This brief description aptly summarizes Huey Richardson's nondescript NFL career after he was taken with the 15th overall selection in the first round during the 1991 NFL Draft. He'll always be known as Chuck Noll's final first-round draft pick. By all accounts and even with their dubious history prior to Noll, Richardson is considered to be among the biggest busts on draft day for the Steelers and in the entire NFL, for that matter. Fortunately for Richardson, he didn't let that define him. Richardson isn't in a class by himself, but when roll is called it's a short list for his NFL career among the biggest first-round busts in the league's history.

The *Pittsburgh Post-Gazette* compiled a list of the Steelers' most notable first-round busts. Here is a selection to go with Richardson:

—DE Daryl Sims, Wisconsin, 20th pick, 1985: The most notable statement he made was when he told the Pittsburgh Press his favorite color was plaid. Lasted two seasons with Steelers.

—G John Rienstra, Temple, 9th, 1986: Jittery player who left team one training camp for mental health reasons. Gone in 1990.

—DE Aaron Jones, Eastern Kentucky, 18th, 1988: Their 10th-round pick that year—OT John Jackson, also from Eastern Kentucky—said they got a better player in him than they did in Jones. And they did. Jackson played 10 seasons in Pittsburgh and 14 in the NFL. Somehow, Jones lasted five years with the Steelers despite being mostly unproductive.

—RB Tim Worley, Georgia, 7th, 1989: Worley ultimately was suspended for the 1992 season because of drug use and was finished in '93. His selection prompted team to pass on Emmitt Smith in '90.

—OT Tom Ricketts, Pitt, 24th, 1989: Called "natural" left tackle, but he could not play the position. Moved to guard and lasted three seasons. NFL career ended in 1993.

—OT Jamain Stephens, North Carolina A&T, 29th, 1996: Steelers' plan to have him sit and watch as a rookie turned into an extended plan. Stephens was gone after the first day of training camp in 1999.

You Can Go Home Again

After a college football career at North Carolina State, followed by stints as a player with the Philadelphia Eagles and Cleveland Browns and time spent as an assistant coach with the Browns and Kansas City Chiefs, Pittsburgh native William Laird Cowher was hired in 1992 to be the head coach for his hometown Steelers.

Bill Cowher was born May 8, 1957, and raised in the Pittsburgh suburb of Crafton, Pennsylvania. He was dressed smartly in a suit and tie during his opening press conference and not yet 35 years old when he first addressed the Steelers media. That appearance probably was the last time he dressed that way for a media event. For nearly each one thereafter, especially during the weekly in-season sessions on Tuesdays, Cowher generally wore a brightly colored sweater. He also was more relaxed during his later years, as opposed to being "a little arrogant" during his debut, by his own account. However, Cowher was also excited on that first day to be coming home.

"When I had the opportunity to follow Chuck Noll, I knew I was coming to a team that knew how to work, how to prepare and how to win," Cowher said during his retirement press conference. "But you don't even try to compare yourself to a man like Chuck Noll, and I haven't even come close to doing the things that he did. And no one will. He was one of a kind. So, you don't even put yourself in that shadow. So, I was very fortunate to be in that situation."

The Cowher Era began with the Steelers in 1992, when the team opened the season against its AFC Central Division rivals, the Houston Oilers, at the Astrodome. The Oilers were favored to win the division that season, since the Steelers appeared to be in a state of flux with a new coach on the sideline for the first time since 1968 and a new starting quarterback in Neil O'Donnell. He beat out incumbent Bubby Brister in an extremely close preseason battle. Sure, there were several holdovers on a solid defensive unit, including future Hall-of-Famer Rod Woodson at cornerback, but that group mostly was relatively unproven as well.

So Cowher, the youngest NFL head coach when he was hired—ironically, the same age as Houston quarterback Warren Moon—would have to pull out all the stops for the Steelers to begin the Cowher Era with a victory in the Astrodome, since the team had not won a regular-season game there in three tries since 1988. This type of game plan was much different than the one primarily used by Noll and his offensive staff, but it was quite necessary.

"You have to do it your way, and you have to be yourself," Cowher said. "There's no blueprint to being a head coach. . . . You have to be yourself, because every situation is different. All you can do is respect your [assistant] coaches and players, and you'll have more good times than bad."

The Steelers rallied from an early 14-0 deficit in that Oilers game thanks, in part, to the riverboat gambler in Cowher. With a defensive background, Cowher took an uncharacteristic chance during his debut when he called for a fake by punter Mark Royals.

The Steelers drove near midfield after the Oilers' second touchdown, and Cowher believed a spark was needed to get his team back in the game. However, he noted that after quarterback Neil O'Donnell was sacked, he called off the fake punt. Neither Royals nor the special teams coach got the message, because Royals took off on fourth-and-long and still ran for a first down. The Steelers eventually scored on that drive and despite trailing 24-16 at halftime, they rallied for 13 second-half points to win, 29-14, in Cowher's opening game. O'Donnell threw a fourth-quarter touchdown pass to secure the victory.

The Steelers went on to win the AFC Central Division crown in 1992 for the first time since 1984 with an 11-5 record. While the team enjoyed new-found success, Cowher was recognized by the Associated Press as the NFL's Coach of the Year, and six Steelers played in the Pro Bowl, the most in more than a decade. Under Cowher, the Steelers became the first AFC team since the 1970 merger to win a 10th division title. Their 11-5 record equaled the best in the conference and gave the Steelers home-field advantage throughout the playoffs. However, in the first postseason game at Three Rivers in exactly 10 years, the Steelers were defeated by eventual AFC champion Buffalo, 24-3.

In 1993, the Steelers earned a wild-card playoff berth, marking their first consecutive playoff appearances since the 1983-84 seasons. A 9-7 record was good for second place in the division, but the season ended in a 27-24 overtime loss at Kansas City in the AFC wild-card matchup with the Chiefs. The 1994 Steelers won seven of their final eight regular-season games for their strongest finish since 1978. They captured a second division title in three years with the AFC's best record of 12-4. After a 29-9 victory over the Cleveland Browns in the first round of the playoffs, Pittsburgh played host to its first AFC championship game since 1979. The game went down to the wire, but the Steelers lost to the San Diego Chargers, 17-13.

With that loss as motivation, the Steelers came on strong the following season. And at 38, Cowher became the youngest head coach to lead his team to a Super Bowl following the 1995 season. The Steelers also captured their third AFC Central Division title in four years, made a fourth straight playoff appearance and won the franchise's first AFC title since 1979. After a first-round bye, the Steelers defeated the Buffalo Bills (40-21) and Indianapolis Colts (20-16) to set up a Super Bowl matchup against the Dallas Cowboys. The Steelers had beaten the Cowboys for two Lombardi trophies in the 1970s and had another shot at them in Super Bowl XXX in Tempe, Arizona. This time, the Cowboys got off to a fast start, Steelers quarterback Neil O'Donnell threw three interceptions, and the franchise lost its first Super Bowl, 27-17.

In 1996, the Steelers finished 10-6 and earned their fifth consecutive trip to the playoffs. Cowher ended the season with

57 career victories, which ranked him second to Noll as a Steelers head coach. The Steelers captured their fourth consecutive AFC Central title in 1997 with an 11-5 record, but they fell one play short from earning a sixth Super Bowl appearance. The Steelers lost to Denver, 24-21, in the AFC championship game at Three Rivers Stadium. In 1998, the Steelers finished a disappointing 7-9 after losing their last five regular-season games and missed the playoffs for the first time under Cowher. The Steelers suffered their second consecutive losing season in 1999, when their record plummeted to 6-10. It was a rough way to finish the 1990s, especially after what the Steelers accomplished under Cowher early on.

The players certainly appreciated what Cowher did for them. Cowher was a players' coach, to be sure, and he was extremely emotional. He certainly brought out the best in his players. Most would do anything for him. All-Pro guard Alan Faneca gave credit to Cowher for leading the Steelers wherever they went. Inside linebacker Larry Foote praised him as well.

"What I'll miss most is his passion," Foote said. "Certain coaches and certain people, when they give speeches, you're not really listening to them. But the one thing I give him a lot of credit for is the tight ship that he ran. You see teams have disappointing seasons, and they fall apart, but Coach Cowher kept a tight ship. Players weren't fighting with each other, not going off on coaches in the media. That's a credit to him, and it's why we respect him the most."

Cowher's opening three draft picks were long-time NFL players. His opening first-round selection was University of Miami offensive tackle Leon Searcy, and he played for the Steelers from 1992-95. But he got a huge free-agent contract with the Jacksonville Jaguars before the 1996 season and played five seasons with them before ending his career with the Baltimore Ravens in 2001.

The Steelers took Clemson inside linebacker Levon Kirkland (1992-2000) in the second round and got Colorado nose tackle Joel Steed (1992-99) in the third. The Steelers also took Penn State safety Darren Perry (1992-98) in the eighth round. Free-agent signings that season included UCLA offensive guard Duval Love (1992-94), Colorado safety Solomon Wilcots (1992), Winston-Salem State wideout Yancey Thigpen (1992-97), and Miami, Florida, running back Albert Bentley (1992), but he played seven more seasons with the Indianapolis Colts.

Cowher teamed with the Steelers' director of football operations, Tom Donahoe, and the scouting staff to secure the draft picks in the 1990s. And they were quite successful. After a strong 1992 draft, the Steelers had a big 1993 as well. Colorado cornerback Deon Figures (1993-96) was their No. 1 pick in 1993, while college teammate Chad Brown was taken in the second round. He played linebacker for the Steelers from 1993-96 and returned in 2006. Georgia wideout Andre Hastings (1993-96) was the third-round selection, while Western Carolina cornerback Willie Williams (1993-96, 2004-05) came on board in the sixth round. The Steelers took Pitt quarterback Alex Van Pelt in the eighth round, but he eventually was released. Van Pelt was a career backup for 11 seasons, including one with the Kansas City Chiefs and the final 10 with the Buffalo Bills (1994-2003). He made three starts in 1997 and eight in 2001. The Steelers were able to release Van Pelt because they signed Ohio State quarterback Mike Tomczak in free agency. He was a part-time starter from 1993-99. They also signed Auburn outside linebacker Kevin Greene (1993-95), who was among the NFL sack leaders, and Mississippi State defensive end Kevin Henry (1993-2000). Both were starters on the Steelers.

The club's No. 1 pick in 1994, Colorado wideout Charles Johnson, played for the Steelers from 1994-98. But he rarely was that big-play threat the team coveted. Johnson tallied 38 catches during each of his opening two NFL seasons but just three touchdowns as a rookie and none in his second season. His best seasons were 1996 and '98 with 60 and 65 receptions, respectively, and he accumulated 1,008 yards (16.8 average) with just three scores in 1996. During the 1998 season he had the most touchdowns with seven. Johnson played two seasons with Philadelphia (1999-2000) and ended a nine-year NFL career with the New England Patriots in 2001 and Buffalo Bills in 2002, but he started just two games for the Pats and none for the Bills after recording 58 for the Steelers and 27 for Philly. Johnson had 354 career catches for 4,606 yards (13.0) and 24 touchdowns, but he never lived up to being a No. 1 pick.

With the second pick that year, the Steelers selected Clemson defensive end Brentson Buckner. He played for the club from 1994-96, but was more well-known for his voracious appetite and custom-made Mercedes Benz with a black-and-gold interior and his number, 96, stitched into the seats, than he was for his play on the field. Buckner was a jovial sort and well-liked by his teammates, but the Steelers put him on a weight limit that he struggled with from the outset. Buckner told reporters that he was despondent after the Steelers lost in the Super Bowl after the 1995 season. He returned home for the offseason, and his mom cooked all his favorite Southern dishes. Buckner ate himself out of a new contract and stayed just one more year in Pittsburgh. He eventually matured and ended a 12-year NFL career with the Cincinnati Bengals (1997), San Francisco 49ers (1998-2000) and Carolina Panthers (2001-2005). Since retiring as a player, Buckner has attempted to secure an NFL coaching position and finally did so as a defensive line coach with the Arizona Cardinals in 2013 for head coach Bruce Arians. Buckner was a coaching intern with the Steelers for several seasons, while Arians was the offensive coordinator.

A big, strong, and mean-looking outside linebacker from Oklahoma State, Jason Gildon was the Steelers' third-round pick in 1994. He played 10 seasons with the Steelers (1994-2003) and was their all-time sack leader when he left for one final season with the Jacksonville Jaguars in 2004. Gildon finished his NFL tenure with 80 career sacks. The Steelers also selected starting safety Myron Bell from Michigan State in the fifth round (1994-97, 2000-01) and signed free-agent running back Fred McAfee from Mississippi College (1994-98).

The Steelers also signed a new play-by-play announcer in 1994, as local legend Bill Hillgrove took over for Jack Fleming and joined even more of a legend, Myron Cope, in the broadcast booth. Hillgrove already had a lengthy announcing career for the Pitt Panthers football and men's basketball programs, and he had a long career as a sports anchor for WTAE-TV in Pittsburgh as well. He still announces games for the Steelers and University of Pittsburgh.

Cowher and Donahoe secured several starters during the 1995 NFL Draft, including Washington tight end Mark Bruener (1995-2003) with their first-round pick. He had a 14-year NFL career, including nine with the Steelers and five with the Houston Texans (2004-2008), but Bruener was a devastating blocker and used more like an additional offensive lineman than a receiving threat. He never had more than the 26 receptions he recorded during his rookie season.

The Steelers' early second-round pick in 1995 was Colorado quarterback Kordell Stewart, who already was well-known for a 64-yard touchdown pass to wideout Michael Westbrook to beat Michigan, 27-26, in Ann Arbor. It was the second touchdown in the final 2:16 by Stewart's Buffaloes, and the winning pass appeared to travel some 70 yards in the air. Stewart played for the Steelers from 1995-2002, first as a Slash—quarterback/running back/receiver—and then as their starting quarterback for six seasons. However, despite displaying toughness and amazing athletic ability that led to regular-season success, Stewart lost two AFC championship games at home, eventually was moved to receiver and replaced by pass-happy, immobile Tommy Maddox. Stewart spent one season with the Chicago Bears and ended his NFL career with the Baltimore Ravens (2004-5). Stewart completed nearly 56 percent of his career passes for 14,746 yards, 77 touchdowns, and 84 interceptions, but he also ran for nearly 3,000 yards (5.1 average) and 38 more scores. He had an 80-yard run in 1996 and a 74-yard jaunt in 1997. There also was a 56-yarder in 1998, one for 45 yards in 2000 and another for 48 in 2001. Stewart also had 41 career receptions for a 16-yard average and five touchdowns with a 71-yard scoring catch in 1995 and 48-yarder in 1996.

The Steelers also selected Nebraska offensive guard Brenden Stai in the third round in 1995 (1995-99) and Georgia Tech safety Lethon Flowers in the fifth round (1995-2002). Free-agent signings included Tennessee State cornerback Randy Fuller (1995-97) and North Texas State running back Erric Pegram (1995-96). Pegram was a part-time starter, and Fuller knocked away Jim Harbaugh's Hail Mary pass attempt to secure the Steelers' win against the Colts in the AFC championship game after the 1995 season. That put the Steelers in the Super Bowl for the first time under Cowher and was the franchise's first appearance in the big game since the 1979 season.

The Steelers had been looking for that powerful, dominating running back for the better part of two decades, and they finally secured him during a draft-day trade with the St. Louis Rams in 1996. Jerome Bettis joined the Steelers and stayed from

1996-2005 after three seasons with the Rams. Bettis capped an amazing career by being part of the franchise's fifth Super Bowl victory after the 2005 season. He completed a spectacular NFL career with 13,662 yards rushing and 91 touchdowns. Bettis was a finalist for the Pro Football Hall of Fame in 2012 and '13 and should be inducted sometime soon. He is sixth on the NFL's all-time rushing list behind Emmitt Smith, Walter Payton, Barry Sanders, Curtis Martin, and LaDainian Tomlinson.

The Steelers also signed Pitt product Jim Sweeney to a free-agent contract, and he played for them from 1996-99. The club was less productive during the actual 1996 NFL Draft. With their No. 1 pick, the Steelers took somewhat of a reach to get massive North Carolina A&T offensive tackle Jamain Stephens. He lasted just three forgettable seasons, 1996-98, and is considered to be among the team's biggest draft-day busts. He came to training camp unprepared and out of shape twice, in 1996 and 1998, with a performance during the run test on opening day in the latter year the last straw for Cowher. Stephens was unceremoniously cut later that day after a poor showing in the run test.

The club's other 1996 draft picks included Penn State fullback Jon Witman in the third round (1996-2001), Florida A&M linebacker Earl Holmes in the fourth round (1996-2001) and Florida State defensive end Orpheus Roye in the sixth round (1996-99, 2008). The No. 1 pick in 1997, Maryland cornerback Chad Scott, quickly earned a starting role and played for the Steelers from 1997-2004. However, he suffered a season-ending knee injury early in 1998 and was much-maligned during his remaining years in Pittsburgh. He never had more than five interceptions in a season, which he had twice (2000-2001). Ohio State's Mike Vrabel was the club's third-round pick, but the Steelers tried to make the college D-lineman a linebacker.

He never panned out and stayed only through his rookie contract (1997-2000). Vrabel left for the Patriots and thrived for eight seasons. He helped them win three Super Bowls in four years and completed a 14-year NFL career with the Kansas City Chiefs (2009-10). The club also signed Michigan State wideout Courtney Hawkins to a free-agent contract that year, and he played for them from 1997-2000.

The Steelers secured three long-time starters, including two perennial Pro Bowlers, during the 1998 NFL Draft. They selected LSU offensive lineman Alan Faneca in the first round (1998-2007), Arizona State defensive lineman Jeremy Staat in the second round (1998-2000), Georgia quarterback Hines Ward in the third round (1998-2011)—but he would be a spectacular wideout for the Steelers—and Alabama cornerback Deshea Townsend in the fourth round (1998-2008). Faneca earned nine Pro Bowl selections and was a nine-time All-Pro at left guard, but he left the Steelers in a bitter contract dispute after the 2007 season. He played two years for the New York Jets and one with the Arizona Cardinals to end his career after the 2010 season. Ward eventually should be inducted in the Hall of Fame after tallying 1,000 career catches for 12,083 yards and 85 touchdowns. He was a four-time Pro Bowl selection, three-time All-Pro, two-time Super Bowl champion, and Super Bowl XL MVP. Townsend was a full-time starter four seasons in Pittsburgh and an excellent extra defensive back the other years, but he always was among their top players in secondary coverage. He had 21 career interceptions.

Staat's stormy three-year tenure in Pittsburgh mirrored the relationship between Cowher and Donahoe, who was instrumental in drafting him. The 1999 NFL Draft would be Donahoe's last, as he was forced to resign after that season. Staat was gone in 2000 as well, as the divide between Cowher and Donahoe turned into a chasm. Cowher clearly won the power struggle and would have more say in personnel matters in the future. The 1999 NFL Draft was the last one the two worked together, and the collaboration missed during the early rounds. No. 1 pick Troy Edwards, a wideout from Louisiana Tech, caught 98 passes for the Steelers from 1999-2001. However, poor work habits and decreased production led to his demise in Pittsburgh and brief stays with three other NFL teams as well. He never matched the 61 catches and five touchdowns he had as a rookie with the Steelers in 1999, and he finished with 203 receptions for 2,404 yards and 11 measly touchdowns in a seven-year career. Weber State free safety Scott Shields was their second-round pick, and he remained just two miserable seasons (1999-2000).

There were two third-round picks, and at least the Steelers hit on one of them with Colorado State pass-rusher Joey Porter (1999-2006). The Steelers made him an outside linebacker, and the enigmatic Porter was a team leader from the beginning to the end of his career before several knee surgeries and a ballooning salary forced his release. Kris Farris, an offensive tackle from UCLA, was a consensus All-American and Outland Trophy winner in college. But in the NFL, the Steelers realized, he was too slow and soft to make it. He lasted one season with the Steelers and one with the Buffalo Bills before moving on to his life's work. In the fourth round, the Steelers found another gem in Northern Colorado defensive end Aaron Smith. He anchored the left side of the defensive line for the Steelers from 1999-2011, but several injuries in his final years ended his career after 13 seasons. He retired as one of the more popular players in the locker room. Nebraska place-kicker Kris Brown was solid from 1999-2001 after being drafted in the seventh round, but they allowed him to leave when his contract expired.

The other 1999 picks had limited to no contribution to the Steelers during their tenures.

Third-round pick Amos Zereoue, a running back from West Virginia, played for the Steelers from 1999-2003. He ran for 762 yards and four touchdowns in 2002 and also caught 42 passes that year, but the speedy Zereoue never became the featured back the Steelers desired.

When Cowher resigned after the 2006 season, his mentor, Marty Schottenheimer, said the young coach was so relentless in pursuing the defensive coordinator position in 1989 that he eventually hired him. Cowher thanked Schottenheimer for giving him a start in coaching and the Rooneys for taking a chance on hiring him as the head coach for the Steelers. He rarely reflected during his time with the club, but that's what his final news conference was all about.

"We've had some disappointments, the AFC championship games when we got so close, but I can honestly say that was the fuel that brought me back and made me appreciate things," Cowher said, referring to his 2-4 record in AFC title games. That was his most substandard work through 15 seasons, but there were far more positive aspects to his head coaching tenure with the Steelers.

During those 15 seasons with the Steelers, eight less than his predecessor Noll, Cowher tied an NFL record by opening his coaching career with six straight playoff appearances. And he led the Steelers to the postseason on 10 occasions overall. They played in six AFC title games, including an amazing five at home, and went to Super Bowls after the 1995 and 2005 seasons with a victory—the franchise's fifth overall—in Super Bowl XL on Feb. 6, 2006 after a stunning 4-0 playoff run as the sixth seed with all games played on the road. Cowher ended his coaching career with a 161-99-1 record, including an 8-8 mark in his final season (2006) and 12-9 record in the postseason. Cowher ranked third in winning percentage among NFL coaches during the 15 years since he took over in 1992, but he probably never realized that he would be that successful when his coaching career began in the Houston Astrodome.

Too Much, Too Fast

Fame and fortune came like lightning in a thunderstorm for Jamain Stephens, as he quickly ascended from Division I-AA North Carolina Agricultural and Technical State University (N.C. A&T) in Greensboro, North Carolina, to the biggest stage in professional football when the Pittsburgh Steelers selected him with the 29th overall pick in the first round during the 1996 NFL Draft.

Stephens' story is all-too familiar to NFL fans. Stephens played for the Steelers from 1996-98, but he was released on the first day of training camp in 1999. He signed with the Cincinnati Bengals that year and stayed with them until 2002. Stephens started 15 of 40 NFL games, including 10 starts in 11 games for the Steelers in 1998. So, his NFL career could be described as rather nondescript, and it all began when the Steelers brought Stephens to Pittsburgh. He became the first football player from North Carolina A&T to be selected in the first round during the NFL Draft, and this elevated status clearly affected Stephens. He appeared to take his foot off the accelerator once he "made it" in the NFL.

Stephens didn't play any games during his rookie season, and he got in half of them with one start in 1997. But it was a struggle from the start, and he did not appear to be prepared for a camp-opening run test—which Steelers coach Bill Cowher instituted since his arrival in 1992—that featured 14 sets of 40-yard dashes with a time limit. Stephens ran with the linemen, got through the test and then laid on the grass at Saint Vincent College in Latrobe, Pennsylvania, where the team holds preseason training camp. That prompted Steelers linebacker Greg Lloyd to wave a white towel over him.

The following season, Stephens came to training camp in great shape and paced his group in Cowher's run test. He also started 10 of 11 games at right tackle when Justin Strzelczyk was injured, appeared to improve as the season wore on and held his own against Green Bay Packers Hall-of-Famer Reggie White in one game.

But the Steelers finished a disappointing 7-9 that season after reaching the AFC championship game the year before, and Cowher wasn't a happy camper when he arrived at training camp in 1999. The Steelers penciled in Stephens at right tackle, but in the spring, they signed veteran Anthony Brown—who started five games the previous season for the Bengals—as a free agent to compete for the job with Stephens and second-year draft pick Chris Conrad. Conditions were horrible for the 1999 test. The sun was bright. There was no shade, and the temperature rose to a skin-baking 92 degrees. And Stephens clearly wasn't prepared for the experience. Generously listed at 6-foot-6 and 330 pounds, Stephens couldn't keep pace with his group and eventually sat on a water cooler after the 11th run. Some teammates surrounded him and urged him to continue, so Stephens got up and walked through two more 40-yarders. Cowher screamed: "Everybody up" during this time—his signature call that practice or in this case, the run test, was over—but many Steelers ignored the call and still encouraged Stephens to finish. It wasn't a pretty sight, as Stephens wobbled through those 40-yarders, but he never ran any more. And Cowher never gave him credit for completing the test.

The Steelers also worked out Stephens on the defensive line, and he appeared to play pretty well. But he clearly was only going to be given a shot to play offensive tackle. To Stephens's credit, he returned for the 1999 season to give it another shot to play right tackle for the Steelers. To be fair, he was scheduled to make $801,500 that season, so he had some incentive. And if he'd been in the same shape that he was in for the previous camp, Stephens likely could have secured the starting job. But all that melted away in the summer heat at Latrobe. Cowher and Tom Donahoe, the Steelers director of football operations, met that fateful night—July 30, 1999—and decided to release their former No. 1 pick.

"He certainly isn't anywhere near where he was a year ago," Cowher said when asked about Stephens after practice. "So, that was very disappointing. To me, it's a great indicator. It's an indicator of where people are. It's an indicator of the preparation that's been done prior to getting here, and it's an indicator of where you need to be."

The Steelers also released a brief statement after Stephens was let go.

"While there were several factors involved in Jamain's release, it was obvious [that] he lacked the commitment to compete in this camp. I had no choice but to release him," Cowher said. "Our expectations are to win a championship, and we will be committed to achieving that goal."

Steelers safety Lee Flowers explained why he and his teammates urged Stephens to complete the run test during his final training camp with the Steelers.

"We're going to run as a team, [and] we're going to die as a team," Flowers said. "We were just trying to help a guy out.

He made it. The whole thing is it's not what times you make as long as you finish, and he finished (the test). And that's the most important thing."

Steelers linebacker Levon Kirkland addressed his comments directly to the inquisitive reporters in attendance.

"You guys are down on him, [but] he's got to know his teammates are behind him," Kirkland said.

Brown, brought in to compete with Stephens, eventually started 11 of the 16 games in 1999. Conrad started three games, while Strzelczyk did not play, as the Steelers stumbled from third to fourth in the AFC Central Division with a 6-10 record. It was the second of three straight seasons where the Steelers would miss the playoffs, and some called for Cowher to be fired. There clearly were personnel issues, as Cowher and Donahoe clashed in a power struggle.

There also were several issues in the Steelers locker room. One incident included running back Richard Huntley, who was Stephens's roommate during his stay at training camp in 1998. Huntley is famous, or maybe the correct word is infamous, for an incident later during his time with the Steelers. After a particularly rough mini-camp practice in June at Three Rivers Stadium when Huntley mixed it up with linebacker Earl Holmes, the two went at it again in the locker room with several media in attendance. Jason Gildon also got involved, as a small wooden locker stool was swung like a Terrible Towel. Fortunately, beefy running back Chris Fuamatu-Ma'afala snatched it from behind, and cooler heads eventually prevailed. Stephens wasn't part of that mess, but that's an example of the Steelers' odd locker room mix. Stephens already had moved on to the Bengals.

Stephens started two of the seven games he played for Cincinnati in 1999 and also opened two games out of nine played in 2001. He played in just five games in 2000 and did not play for the Bengals during his final NFL season in 2002. So, that was it for Stephens in the NFL. Steelers management said that Stephens has contacted them to discuss an attempted comeback. He was seen at the club's training camp in 2012 and would be some five months from his 40th birthday if he attempted to participate at camp in 2013 as well.

If his unlikely comeback attempt doesn't pan out, all Steelers fans are likely to remember about Stephens are his two failed running tests for Cowher in 1997 and 1999 and the humiliating release of the former first-round pick several hours after the second one.

A Square Peg in a Round Hole

Even though he looked the part as a 6-foot-6, 295-pound bull-strong young man at 21 years old, Jeremy Staat never seemed to fit in after the Steelers selected him with their second-round choice. He starred in track and field, his "first love," and football at Bakersfield (California) High School and spent two years at Bakersfield Junior College before transferring to Arizona State. Staat was an offensive lineman until moving to the D-line for the Sun Devils. He had moderate success as a junior "rush" tackle, but exploded for 9 1/2 sacks, 20 total tackles behind the line, and 67 total stops. The ASU defense, led by Pac-10 defensive player of the year Pat Tillman, who was Staat's best friend, was ranked among the nation's best. So, it basically was potential that led the Steelers to choose Staat so high in the 1998 draft, but neither side knew what it was getting into after that.

"Going into the NFL, you know, I was never a fan of the NFL," Staat said. "I didn't really watch a lot of football or follow football. And I really didn't know anything about the business of football. I was told a little bit about it, but I just figured that the best players would be the guys who were on the field. It seemed simple enough to me. I just thought that the best guys would get to play, but I found out pretty quick that things didn't work that way. And I ran into a bunch of guys who were just milking the system. They said things like: 'I've got a five-year contract for $25 million, regardless of my play, so I'll still get paid.'

"They didn't think they could be released, because the team had too much money invested in them in a signing bonus. So, I was kind of ignorant to all this. I never heard guys talk about this, all that money, and then there was the team's side of it. After I was released by Pittsburgh, I really saw the full effect of the beast that the NFL could be as far as everybody trying to hold onto their job, unless you're an owner. So, I never realized that there was the player's side and there was the owner's side, management's side. I just thought we all worked together for the team. Unfortunately, those two sides don't see eye to eye. And the player usually loses in that situation."

Staat said several times that he didn't regret his spotty NFL career, which officially lasted just 32 games. However, it was enough to qualify him for a pension, and it also allowed Staat to move on to bigger, better, and more fulfilling ventures. A few years after Tillman's death in Afghanistan in 2004, Staat joined the U.S. Marine Corp. and reached the rank of Lance Cpl. Staat, who was playing in the Arena Football League at the time, was among the 300 soldiers in the 1st Battalion, 3rd Marine Regiment deployed in 2007 from Kaneohe Bay, Hawaii, to Iraq for seven months.

"The way I look at it, we're spreading freedom, and you have to support the troops, and you have to support the war," Staat told a Honolulu TV station. "You can't just tell some Marine who just lost his buddy that we supported you but not the war, because in that case you're basically saying to that Marine that his buddy just died for nothing. We're one team . . . I never felt right about making the money I was making. We pay millions to professional athletes and entertainers, yet we pay military service people pennies to a dollar, and they're the ones risking their lives."

Tillman, who played defensive back for the Arizona Cardinals, turned down a three-year, $3.6 million contract to join the U.S. Army Rangers. He was killed by friendly fire near the Pakistan-Afghanistan border in 2004. Tillman's family initially was told that enemy fire killed him, which drew the ire of many Americans, including Staat and spurred him to join the war efforts as well. After his Iraqi deployment as a machine gunner, Staat returned home and discovered a heart condition. He had to retire from the military for medical considerations and eventually was honorably discharged. Eventually, Staat and his wife, Janelle, began the Jeremy Staat Foundation. Through the non-profit organization, Staat is hopeful that he can increase awareness for military veterans. Specifically, his focus is veteran suicide awareness, as well as the promotion of other veteran organizations and veteran centers on college campuses across the United States. Staat also took part in a cross-country bicycle trip that began at the Bakersfield, Calif. Wall of Valor and ended at the Vietnam Veterans Memorial Wall in Washington, D.C. The journey lasted several months in 2012.

"When I look back at my athletic career—high school, junior college, Division I—and see all the things I accomplished as an athlete, whether it be football or track and field, I have a lot to be proud of," Staat said. "I did pretty well in track and field. I missed out on the Olympic Trials by a foot in the discus when I was 18 years old. What amazes me is that I could come out of a Division I school after playing on the defensive line for just two seasons there before I got drafted by Pittsburgh. Before that, in high school and junior college, I was an offensive tackle, but ASU gave me a scholarship to be a defensive tackle. So, I went for it. I developed as a pass-rusher and did pretty well at ASU. So, the Steelers drafted me, but they played a three-four defense.

"And the D-ends and nose tackle are basically just there to tie up the linemen so the linebackers can make the tackles. I definitely wasn't used to that. I was able to shoot gaps and make plays in the backfield as a senior at ASU, but I couldn't do any of that with the Steelers. It was way different, and I wasn't really a good fit for that system. You know, [defensive coordinator Jim Haslett] said the same thing. He said: 'I know you're not a three-four guy, you're a 4-3 guy who can shoot gaps from the tackle spot, but I can't play you in that type of scheme.' I didn't know how to respond to that, but I said: 'Well, I'm here, so what do you want me to do?' It was really frustrating. I wanted to play, but Coach Haslett told me that I couldn't because I wasn't suited to playing the scheme that they had in Pittsburgh. But they drafted me? In the second round?

"Then, there was the other situation," Staat added. "The Steelers had a GM [Donahoe] who didn't like the head coach [Cowher]. And I was drafted by Donahoe, who eventually was forced out after a power struggle with Cowher. The mistake I made was that I should have followed Donahoe. He went to Buffalo to be the GM there, and I probably could have gotten a huge contract to play for him. But I didn't do that. I wanted to get closer to home because my parents were divorced, and the girl I was dating was all jacked up on drugs. If I could get back home, I thought I could fix it all. . . . So, I chose to go to Seattle, but their Director of Pro Personnel [Will Lewis] just happened to be the brother of the Steelers defensive backs coach [Tim Lewis]. I never had a chance.

"I just wanted to play the game that I loved playing, and I wasn't able to do that. I really believe that the true meaning of the game has been lost for a long time in the NFL, and that's a shame. You know, I signed on with Oakland [after Seattle], and coach Bill Callahan [offensive coordinator in 2001] believed I could be a pulling guard in his offensive system and he could turn me into a Pro Bowl player in just two years. That's when the head coach from Oakland, Chuckie [Jon Gruden], got traded to Tampa [for four draft picks prior to the 2002-03 season]. Callahan said that he had bigger fish to fry, because he got the head coaching job, and that meant I was done in Oakland.

"He told me he would release me in August," Staat added. "So, my agent, Frank Bauer, went to Coach Cowher and asked him if I was better as an offensive guard or defensive tackle. We didn't know what to do at that point. St. Louis wanted to pick me up, but we wanted to tell them a position. It was hard for me to believe, but Coach Cowher came to my aid. He said I had too much fire to play offense, and I had to play on the defensive side of the ball. I guess I took it too personally, but it was just business. So, I ended up playing a few games for St. Louis that year and got my retirement. Then, I got out of the NFL and moved on in my career. [And] if things didn't go the way they did, I wouldn't be where I'm at today, and I love where I'm at today and the people I've met."

Staat believed he could use his myriad of experiences as a former NFL player, U.S. Marine, and motivational speaker to help the youth in America.

"Kids are our future, and they need to be educated with complete honesty about what is ahead for them in life," Staat said. "Through my foundation, I try to motivate and inspire kids. I want to be completely honest with them. I don't want to tell them what they want to hear. I'll tell them how it is out there, what they need to know. I'll tell them the truth, not like some other guys. The NFL isn't as glamorous as some kids might think. I'm 36, and I've done all kinds of things. Sure, I could have spent a long career in the NFL, but I would have missed out on the rest of my 20s and 30s. But I'm glad I didn't do that. I got to experience a lot more, and I stayed healthy. You see some of these guys, and they can't walk. Their hands are all mangled. That's not for me. No way.

"I guess some people in Pittsburgh believed I was a wild and crazy guy, but that was after I knew it was over. I remember talking with Coach Cowher on the sideline one day and asked him when I was going to get a chance to play. He said: 'Do you think you're ready?' I said: 'I know I'm ready.' But I was moved inside, and everybody knew that a 6-foot-6, 295-pound nose tackle just wasn't going to work out. One time, I decided I was going to shoot the gap to make a play. I wanted to make plays like everybody else, and I knocked the back down for about a seven-yard loss. Well, I got my ass chewed out by [defensive line coach] John Mitchell on the sideline because I didn't do what I was supposed to do. I didn't tie up the center and allowed him to get out on the linebacker.

"I guess if I would have missed the tackle, they would have had a big play, but I made the tackle," Staat added. "I was told that I wasn't there to make plays. My job was to keep the center and guard off the linebackers so they could make the plays. No wonder it took Joel Steed nine years to make the Pro Bowl. Joel was a great nose tackle and a great guy. I don't know how he did it all those years. I came from a program where I was allowed to make plays, shooting gaps and making plays in the backfield, but then I got to the Steelers and basically wasn't allowed to go make a play. That doesn't seem right. So, that's why I had a really bad taste in my mouth when I left Pittsburgh."

Staat also had a bad hairdo when he left. He colored his hair to completely blond at one point and then added streaks of various other colors.

"I did that as a way to stand out," Staat said. "I wanted to be different. I wanted to be unique and be seen, because I felt like I was doing a heckuva job and not being recognized for it. During that time, back then, Dennis Rodman was doing a lot of stupid stuff and getting recognition for it. So, I guess I wanted some of that, too. It's funny, after I did it, a lot of other guys were doing it. Junior Seau, he did it, but he was making more money than me. So, he got more publicity over it. So, that's how it goes in the NFL, and it's always going to be that way. [But] I loved the City of Pittsburgh and loved the fans.

"The Steelers fans were terrific, blue-collar people who spent their hard-earned money to come out on Sundays to watch the Steelers play. What a great group of fans. I always wanted to get back there to show my wife the city, maybe meet up with some of the people that I got to know back then. I don't know when I'll be able to do that, but I've wanted to go back for a while now. . . . I talked to more than 100,000 kids last year, and I did it all free of charge to the schools. Maybe I could talk to students in Pittsburgh. All we would need to do was have a fundraiser there to pay for the trip. I'd love to return to Pittsburgh to speak to the students there. That would be great."

And this time, Staat would be much more well-rounded than he was in 1998.

CHAPTER 8

The 2000s

OUT WITH THE OLD . . .

Little did wide receiver Plaxico Burress know that when the Pittsburgh Steelers selected him in the first round with the eighth overall pick during the 2000 NFL Draft, he would make history. Sure, Burress was always confident, and he certainly believed that he would be a success in the league after a strong college career at Michigan State. However, Burress was unaware that he would make a cameo appearance during the final season at Three Rivers Stadium until he signed with the Steelers.

Burress had just 22 catches for 273 yards and no touchdowns as a rookie that season after missing four games due to a hand injury. Burress would have a starring role during the next four seasons with the Steelers, and so did several other draft picks from that 2000 class, including second-round offensive tackle Marvel Smith from Arizona State (2000-08) and fifth-round outside linebacker Clark Haggans from Colorado State (2000-07). Both worked their way into the starting lineup for several seasons. The Steelers also signed New Hampshire fullback Dan Kreider (2000-07) to a free-agent contract. Burress played for the Steelers from 2000-04, the New York Giants from 2005-08 and one season with the New York Jets (2011) before returning to the Steelers in 2012. Burress missed the 2009-10 seasons, because he was in jail after accidentally shooting himself while partying in a New York club. From 2000-07, Burress had three seasons with 60 or more catches and three with 70 or more.

After they started the 2000 season with an 0-3 record, the Steelers rebounded to finish the year at 9-7. But they just missed the playoffs. The 2000 season wasn't distinct for any player or on-field performance. It was all about 30-year-old Three Rivers Stadium, which held its swan song, and the "Fat Lady" definitely was warming up. With Heinz Field, the Steelers' new home, already built just steps away to one side of Three Rivers and ready to go for the following season, 2000 was the farewell performance for Three Rivers Stadium. It opened on July 16, 1970, as the Steelers shared their home with Major League Baseball's Pittsburgh Pirates, who also got a new stadium in 2001 called PNC Park. The Steelers went 4-4 in their final eight games at Three Rivers, but none were as spectacular as the finale on December 16, 2000, as nearly 50 former Steelers were in attendance to represent past teams.

The current players paid tribute to the ex-Steelers by stomping the Washington Redskins, 24-3, in front of 58,183 raucous fans. About the only thing the NFC opponent won that day was the opening coin toss with Steelers Hall-of-Famers Jack Ham, Jack Lambert, Mel Blount, and Franco Harris watching. When the Redskins made the correct call, Lambert let out a piercing scream and did his best to motivate the Steelers. Steelers inside linebacker Levon Kirkland, a defensive captain, was practically gushing while describing the situation.

"Jack just got fired up," an equally emotional Kirkland blurted. "He just said: 'All right, defense. Let's kill. Let's go.' That was great, man. You could see how intense he was. It just made us go out there and play better. . . . To me, it was like the last playoff game at Three Rivers. This was an opportunity to add to the history of this stadium, and I'm real proud of it."

Rookie cornerback Hank Poteat from Pitt keyed a 17-point Steelers outburst in the second quarter when he returned a punt 53 yards for a touchdown. Running back Richard Huntley, who had just one touchdown in the previous 14 games with the Steelers, scored twice against the Redskins to seal the win. It wasn't really a playoff game at Three Rivers, and there wouldn't be another one because the Steelers 9-7 record wasn't good enough to qualify. But there were many other post-season matchups during the 31 NFL seasons at Three Rivers Stadium from 1970-2000. The franchise recorded a fabulous 182-73 record and a .714 winning percentage that included many post-season contests.

"To have the Hall-of-Fame players come back, the alumni to come back and be honored the way they were and to be part of them and see them was a great experience," Steelers tight end Mark Bruener said. "[And] for Mr. Rooney to be as excited as he was and to win the game in the fashion that we did was really special, too. I couldn't have expected a better situation or story line."

Former defensive end L.C. Greenwood wore a bright red Santa hat and his trademark gold football shoes during a post-game ceremony where all the ex-Steelers were introduced. Three Rivers rocked as loudly as ever from start to finish, despite a cold, overcast, and rainy day. The dominating Steelers performance and ensuing fan celebration was nearly as wild as it was for many of the great past games at Three Rivers. The Steelers were overdue for a performance like this. They had not made the playoffs since 1997. The 1999 Steelers were 2-6 at home, and the win against the Redskins stopped a second straight losing record in the building. It was a fitting tribute.

Leading up to the final game at the stadium, a vote was taken by media and fans, and the top 10 games and plays were selected. Here is the list:

The top game was the 1975 AFC championship contest that was dubbed the Ice Bowl, as the Steelers beat the Oakland Raiders, 16-10, January 4, 1976, to advance to the Super Bowl for a second straight year.

The second-best game was the club's first playoff appearance, December 23, 1972, as it edged the Oakland Raiders, 13-7, on Franco Harris' Immaculate Reception, which was the No. 1 play.

The No. 3 game was the AFC championship win against the Indianapolis Colts after the 1995 season. The Steelers sealed a 20-16 victory January 14, 1996, as cornerback Randy Fuller broke up Jim Harbaugh's Hail Mary pass. The defensive gem was the No. 3 play.

A pair of overtime victories against the Cleveland Browns were the fourth and fifth top games. No. 4 was a 33-30 win November 25, 1979, while No. 5 was a 15-9 win September 24, 1978, as tight end Bennie Cunningham ran free in the secondary and caught a flea-flicker pass for a touchdown.

Game No. 6 was a 27-13 victory against the Houston Oilers, January 6, 1980, which sealed a fourth Super Bowl appearance in six years, as Joe Greene slammed Oilers running back Earl Campbell and knocked him for a loop. Greene's play was No. 4 on the list.

The No. 7 game was a 28-10 victory against the Baltimore Colts December 27, 1975, as outside linebacker Andy Russell rambled 93 yards for a touchdown after scooping up a fumble. Russell's jaunt was the No. 7 play.

Top game No. 8 was an overtime win against the Jacksonville Jaguars October 27, 1997, as quarterback Kordell Stewart connected on a shovel pass for a touchdown in the 23-17 OT victory. Stewart's 17-yard scoring pass to running back Jerome Bettis was the No. 8 play.

Another victory against the Cleveland Browns made the list and came in at No. 9. The Steelers won the AFC divisional playoff contest, 29-9, January 7, 1995, but they lost to the San Diego Chargers in the AFC championship game the next week.

Top victory No. 10 was the other AFC championship game victory against the Houston Oilers January 7, 1979, as the Steelers won 34-5.

"Through it all, Three Rivers ended up being a very, very good home for the Pittsburgh Steelers," Greene said. Russell tried to make a parallel to another ancient building.

"It's beyond belief that they're tearing down the stadium 30 years later, and the Coliseum in Rome is still standing," Russell said. Steelers owner Dan Rooney's comment was brief and to the point.

"What a place it was," Rooney said. Dominated by concrete and steel, Three Rivers Stadium wasn't aesthetically beautiful, but it was a sight for sore eyes to the Steelers and their fans when completed in 1970 after the franchise split time between Pitt Stadium and Forbes Field in previous years. And it dressed up pretty well for seven AFC championship games, which included four Steelers victories and performances by countless Pro Bowl players and members of the Pro Football Hall of Fame.

"That stadium was a spectacular place," Russell said. "It was beautiful, as far as I'm concerned. I know some might not have liked the turf, but it was a great place for us to play. And the Steelers fans really made it that way."

Among the last events at Three Rivers Stadium was a concert by the boy band 'N Sync on July 26, 2000. Ironically, the first event held at the Steelers new home, Heinz Field, also was an 'N Sync concert on August 18, 2001. The new stadium enters its second decade, but it remains to be seen if it can come close to Three Rivers as a great home-field advantage for the Steelers.

. . . In with the New

It's appropriate that 6-foot-1, 325-pound Casey Hampton was the Steelers' first-round draft pick in 2001, because the former University of Texas nose tackle anchored the club's defensive line from that season through 2012, just like Mean Joe Greene was the cornerstone of the Steel Curtain when Three Rivers Stadium opened three decades earlier. But that steel-and-cement bowl was long gone by the time Hampton's name was called, and Heinz Field was the Steelers' newest home.

"Coach Cowher said I'm his type of player," Hampton said after the Steelers selected him that season. "I like to compete every play, and I like to win every individual battle. That's how I play every snap."

Steelers long-time defensive line coach John Mitchell believed there was a lot to like about his newest nose tackle.

"There are three things that I really like about him," Mitchell said after the first round and Hampton's selection. "He's a no-nonsense guy, and football is important to him. He's been well-coached. He stays on his feet, and you can't make plays in the NFL without staying on your feet."

The club didn't pad its roster much by using the 2001 NFL Draft, as Georgia linebacker Kendrell Bell, taken in the second round, was the only other significant pick. He only lasted four seasons but was the defensive rookie of the year in 2001. The Steelers were able to add a couple starters and some depth through free agency, however, as nose tackle Chris Hoke from BYU (2001-11), quarterback Tommy Maddox from UCLA (2001-05), center Jeff Hartings from Penn State (2001-06), and safety Mike Logan from West Virginia (2001-06) were signed sometime after the draft and prior to the season. Logan, a native of Pittsburgh suburb McKeesport, Pennsylvania, was thrilled to play for his hometown team after four seasons with the Jacksonville Jaguars.

"This is great," Logan said when the Steelers signed him. "For me to be able to play for the franchise that I've been following since I was a little kid, this is one of the best things to ever happen to me. I'm just so excited to be part of the Pittsburgh Steelers now, and all of my family can come to see me play."

Prior to the Steelers regular-season schedule, the team played a preseason game against the Detroit Lions on August 25, 2001, at Heinz Field. The stadium's unofficial opening game was won by the Steelers, 20-7, with 57,829 in attendance. The first official football game played in the stadium was between the Pitt Panthers and East Tennessee State Sept. 1, and the Panthers won, 31-0, as quarterback David Priestley scored the opening touchdown on an exhilarating 85-yard run. The Steelers' home-opener was scheduled for September 16 against the Cleveland Browns, but due to the heinous terrorist attacks on September 11, all NFL games that week were postponed until the end of the season. Therefore, the club's official first home game was October 7 against the Cincinnati Bengals, and the Steelers recorded a 16-7 victory.

Quarterback Kordell Stewart managed the game pretty well with 15-for-24 passing for 151 yards, no touchdowns, but no interceptions, either. His passing moved the ball when necessary, but the Steelers ran the ball extremely well against the Bengals. Bruising Jerome Bettis tallied 153 yards on 23 carries, while Stewart added 63 rushing yards and a touchdown. Bettis needed just 54 yards to become the 14th player in NFL history to rush for 10,000 career yards. He picked up the necessary yardage on his first five carries and gained 103 yards by halftime. It was his 48th career 100-yard game.

"A lot of times, I wasn't seeing anybody until I got into their secondary," Bettis said, as the Steelers out-rushed the Bengals, 274-65. "Our offensive line was just gouging guys, so it was a matter of me making a guy miss here or running over a guy there."

The opening game at Heinz Field was the Steelers' first home game on grass since 1969, when the franchise shared Forbes Field with Pittsburgh Pirates. The Steelers posted an AFC-best 13-3 regular-season record in 2001, including a 7-1 mark at their new home field, and advanced to the AFC championship game. The Steelers defeated the defending Super Bowl champion Baltimore Ravens, 27-10, in the AFC divisional playoffs. The contest was the first postseason game at Heinz Field. However, they suffered a disappointing 24-17 home loss in the AFC title game to the eventual Super Bowl champion New England Patriots.

A Foundation Is Built

The 2002 season was crucial to the team's development, but not entirely for its on-field accomplishments. After an 0-2 start, the Steelers rallied to make the playoffs for a second consecutive season. However, the team's Super Bowl hopes ended when they lost, 34-31, in overtime to the Tennessee Titans on the road. There were several controversial calls that didn't go the Steelers' way during that game, but there also was a lot of promise for the future, especially after the Steelers' success during the 2002 NFL Draft and with free-agent signings. Six draft picks and four free agents secured in 2002 were key players during the Steelers' successful runs in upcoming seasons.

The team's first-round pick was Auburn offensive guard Kendall Simmons, who became a starter and played for the Steelers from 2002-08. A severe knee injury and the onset of diabetes hampered Simmons later years. In the second round, the Steelers chose Indiana wideout Antwaan Randle El, who had been a quarterback in college. Randle El turned into a solid possession receiver and big-play punt-returner. He remained four years through his rookie contract (2005) and returned in 2010 after four seasons with the Washington Redskins but was ineffective and not re-signed after that.

Florida State safety Chris Hope was the third-round pick, and he eventually became a starter. But after his rookie contract agreement ended (2005), Hope signed a free-agent deal with the Tennessee Titans and spent six seasons there. He played for the Atlanta Falcons in 2012. Another future starter came aboard in the fourth round when Michigan inside linebacker Larry Foote was selected. He played for the Steelers from 2002-08 and signed a free-agent deal with his hometown Detroit Lions in 2009. However, he returned to the Steelers and was a veteran leader from 2010-13.

The only other draft picks to make a strong contribution to the Steelers were Georgia running back Verron Haynes, taken in the fifth round (2002-07), and BYU defensive end Brett Keisel, who was their second pick in the seventh round. Haynes was never more than a backup, but Keisel was a special-teams wedge-buster for several seasons before securing a starting spot at right end. He has played for the Steelers from 2002-2013 and has been a starter since 2006.

The Steelers hit the jackpot in free agency in 2002. They signed Virginia inside linebacker James Farrior from the New York Jets, and he played for the club from 2002-11 as a key starter and defensive captain. They also signed outside linebacker James Harrison, who played on special teams until Joey Porter was released. Harrison, from Kent State, played in 2002 and returned in 2004. He developed into one of the most feared and fierce hitters in the league, as well as the best defensive players. He was the NFL's defensive player of the year in 2008. Harrison wouldn't take a 30-percent pay cut despite getting $20 million guaranteed in his previous contract and was released after the 2012 season.

The Steelers also signed hometown hero Charlie Batch. A quarterback from Eastern Michigan, Batch grew up in Homestead, Pennsylvania, played scholastically for Steel Valley High School and began his NFL career as a starter with the Detroit Lions. He's a gregarious sort who has developed several charities to help the Pittsburgh-area youth, and he was a solid backup quarterback for the Steelers from 2002-12. Place-kicker Jeff Reed, who played collegiately for North Carolina, was a solid performer from 2002-10. However, too many off-field issues and erratic kicking led to his release. He also signed with the San Francisco 49ers in 2010 but has not played in the league since then.

The Steelers began the 2003 season with a 34-15 victory against AFC North rival Baltimore, but they never played that well again that year and finished the season with a 6-10 record. It was the first time in three years that the Steelers missed the playoffs, but they were winners during the NFL Draft that year. The Steelers traded up in the first round to secure Southern Cal safety Troy Polamalu. The Steelers wanted Polamalu so badly that they gave up their third- and sixth-round picks to move from 27th to 16th in the first round. Polamalu has been a starter since his second NFL season (2004) and has two years remaining on his current contract (2013-14).

In the second round, the Steelers selected nearly 6-foot-4, 270-pound Alonzo Jackson from Florida State. He was a rush end in college for two seasons, but the Steelers wanted to move him to outside linebacker. However, he wasn't strong enough or fast enough (4.73 in the 40) to cut it. Jackson spent 2003-04 with the Steelers and then was released. Jackson is among the biggest early round busts in Steelers drafts. The Steelers lost their third-round pick in the move to get Polamalu, but secured another gem in the fourth round despite going to Louisiana-Lafayette for him. Cornerback Ike Taylor has been an integral part of the Steelers defense since then and a starter since 2005. He has been rated among the league's best cornerbacks in recent years.

Franchise QB Finally Secured

Some were calling for Steelers coach Bill Cowher's head and protruding jaw after the club went 6-10 in 2003. However, that horrendous season had one bright spot: it set the Steelers at quarterback for at least the next decade, as the team selected Ben Roethlisberger from Miami (Ohio) with the 11th overall pick in the first round during the 2004 NFL Draft. There were many pretenders for the title of franchise quarterback since Terry Bradshaw officially retired after the 1983 season, but Roethlisberger has a stranglehold on that crown now. He stabilized the quarterback position for the first time in two decades and gave the Steelers a chance to win every time he played. He has been the club's starting quarterback since the third game of his rookie season.

There was a rumor swirling during draft week that Cowher coveted North Carolina State quarterback Philip Rivers, but Steelers management reportedly overruled and chose Roethlisberger. Eli Manning and Rivers were the first and fourth players selected in the first round, respectively, but by teams that would trade them. After making it clear that he wouldn't play for San Diego, Manning was sent from the Chargers to the New York Giants, while Rivers went from the Giants to the Chargers. Both have been with those teams since the draft. Roethlisberger was the third quarterback taken in the first round in 2004, and Tulane's J.P. Losman went to the Buffalo Bills with the 22nd overall pick. With two Super Bowl victories each by Manning and Roethlisberger, some believe the 2004 NFL Draft rivaled the 1983 version.

"When we get done playing, I want them to say that our class was the greatest quarterback class of all time," Roethlisberger said. "Philip Rivers, myself, Eli, and Matt Schaub were in that class. So, of course, you root for the other guys."

Schaub actually was a third-round pick by the Atlanta Falcons in 2004, but he's finally coming into his own with the Houston Texans. Manning is a two-time Super Bowl MVP, having won the award after the 2007 and 2011 seasons.

"It has to be, right?" Roethlisberger said when asked if the 1983 quarterback class was the best. "I don't know, but that's the one I'd put at No. 1. But 2004 is pretty good. The championships [already] in our [class] is a little more than theirs."

The first-round quarterback run in 1983 had John Elway being taken by the Baltimore Colts at No. 1 overall and later traded to Denver, Todd Blackledge by the Kansas City Chiefs at No. 7, Jim Kelly by the Buffalo Bills at No. 14, Tony Eason by the New England Patriots at No. 15, Ken O'Brien by the New York Jets at No. 24, and Dan Marino by the Miami Dolphins at No. 27. Elway, Kelly, and Marino have all been inducted into the Pro Football Hall of Fame.

While Roethlisberger and Manning are far from completing careers that should end with Hall-of-Fame busts for both of them, their draft class might fall one short of the three Hall-of-Famers in the 1983 group. However, that class is just 2-8 in the Super Bowl with Elway collecting both victories. He also has three losses. Kelly was 0-4, while Marino lost his only Super Bowl appearance after his second NFL season. Manning and Roethlisberger have two Super Bowl wins each, so that's a 4-2 edge in that category for the 2004 class. Roethlisberger also has a loss in the big game, but a 4-1 record beats 2-8 every time.

The Steelers also selected future starting left offensive tackle Max Starks (2004-12) from Florida in the third round that year and added several players as free agents, including safety Tyrone Carter from Minnesota (2004-09) and future featured back "Fast" Willie Parker from North Carolina (2004-09).

Tommy "Gun" Maddox began 2004 as the Steelers' starting quarterback, but after an opening win against the Oakland Raiders at Heinz Field he got roughed up by the Baltimore Ravens on the road in Game 2. Since Maddox was out for an extended period, the Steelers needed to decide whether to play Brian St. Pierre or Roethlisberger, who they had hoped could watch and learn as a rookie. The Steelers decided to throw Roethlisberger into the fire.

Still, there were mixed feelings among Roethlisberger's teammates. All-Pro guard Alan Faneca wasn't too kind a few days before the quarterback's first start when asked how he felt about having a rookie lead the offense.

"How would you like to have a young kid go to work with you?" Faneca replied to the reporters. "It's not really exciting for us or something we're looking forward to right now."

Steelers offensive coordinator Ken Whisenhunt believed that Roethlisberger would play some as a rookie but not be a starter. He wanted the quarterback to be brought along slowly, like his mentor Joe Gibbs did with his young guys with the Washington Redskins, even though Roethlisberger wanted to play. But the quarterback deferred to Cowher and the staff on his first day with the Steelers.

"I'm more than willing to do whatever it is that Coach asks of me and what's best for the team, whether that's coming in and playing right now or learning behind Tommy for a little while," Roethlisberger said on draft day. "Whatever the team asks of me and is best for the team, I'm more than willing to do. The big thing is, if Tommy is willing to do it, I would like to learn as much as I can from him being a veteran and the quarterback that he is. I'm more than willing to learn everything that he's willing to teach me."

Hurricane Jeanne forced Roethlisberger's first start to be postponed until Sunday night, September 26 at Miami, but it wasn't an ill wind blowing for the Steelers. Both teams played good defense, but the Steelers were a little better from the opening kick. Several first-half downpours, caused by remnants from the hurricane, left standing water in the baseball infield, which made footing especially treacherous there. The start of the second half was delayed so the grounds crew could dry the field and apply additional bags of dirt.

"That was the worst weather I ever played in," Steelers wideout Hines Ward said, but that didn't stop he and his teammates from moving the ball. Still, neither quarterback could throw the football efficiently.

"The weather in the first half was not conducive to doing anything," Steelers coach Bill Cowher said. "We couldn't even hold onto the ball. Both teams couldn't throw it. But that's the kind of football I love."

Cowher especially had to love his defense. It held the Dolphins to 169 total yards and bruised more than just their pride. A jarring tackle by Steelers free safety Chris Hope sent running back Lamar Gordon from the game with an injured left shoulder and his replacement, Leonard Henry, was knocked backward by a big hit from inside linebacker James Farrior. It later was determined that Gordon had a dislocated shoulder and was ruled out for the season. Even before the heaviest rain, the Steelers forced three turnovers on Miami's first seven plays. The crowd was small—reportedly about half Steelers fans among the 30,000 estimated in attendance—but it vociferously booed Miami quarterback A.J. Feeley, the Dolphins offense and the play-calling.

The Steelers got a 40-yard field goal from place-kicker Jeff Reed nearly seven minutes into the first quarter, as Roethlisberger hooked up with wide receiver Plaxico Burress for a 42-yard gain to set it up. Burress made a diving catch on the play, but there wasn't much more action in the first half. Trailing 3-0 early in the second half, Miami coach Dave Wannstedt gambled with a quarterback sneak on fourth-and-one at the Miami 47, but Feeley was stopped for no gain. Six plays later, Reed hit a 51-yard field goal.

Miami's best drive covered 44 yards to set up a 34-yard Olindo Mare field goal 1:35 into the fourth quarter to make it 6-3. But Roethlisberger, who was intercepted on his first pass as a starter, kept battling. He guided a Steelers drive midway through the fourth quarter that reached the 7-yard line, and the rookie looked for the end zone on the next play. He connected with Ward for the touchdown, and the Roethlisberger era was off to a flying start.

"It wasn't pretty, at times, but we got the win," Roethlisberger said.

TIME FOR A CHANGE

After 15 seasons, Bill Cowher resigned as the Steelers head coach. The January 5, 2007, announcement surprised many and set off a coaching search by the franchise for just the third time in nearly four decades. Cowher finally led the Steelers to a fifth Super Bowl victory, and he finished with a 161-99-1 record. That was second to Chuck Noll's total in 23 seasons.

The Steelers interviewed several coaches, including two of their own assistants—Pittsburgh native Russ Grimm, their offensive line coach, and offensive coordinator Ken Whisenhunt—as well as one-year Minnesota Vikings defensive coordinator Mike Tomlin. Whisenhunt made a preemptive strike and accepted an offer to be the Arizona Cardinals head coach. The Steelers hired 34-year-old Mike Tomlin on January 22, 2007, to be their third head coach since 1969. Grimm eventually was hired by Whisenhunt to coach the Cardinals O-line. Tomlin was the first African-American head coach in the Steelers' 74-year history.

Steelers president Art Rooney II said Tomlin planned to focus on stopping the run, playing physical on defense, and running the ball successfully on offense.

"He wants to play the kind of football the Pittsburgh Steelers want to play," Rooney II said during Tomlin's opening press conference. "He wants to play the kind of football Steelers fans have come to appreciate."

Tomlin's initial NFL Draft with the Steelers yielded two future starting linebackers when the club took Florida State's Lawrence Timmons in the first round (2007-13) and Michigan's LaMarr Woodley in the second round (2007-13). Timmons has played inside linebacker, while Woodley has been a pass-rusher on the outside. And in the fifth round, the Steelers took Louisville cornerback William Gay (2007-11). He played for the Arizona Cardinals in 2012, but re-signed with the Steelers for 2013. The Steelers also signed Clemson defensive end Nick Eason in free agency, and he was a key backup from 2007-10.

"His football character is what we seek," Tomlin said about Timmons. "He loves the game of football. He's very versatile. His skill set defies scheme, which is some of the things that we've talked about. He's an outside backer, but he's capable of playing off the line of scrimmage and on the tight end. He has pass-rush capabilities. But he has the RH factor. He's a runner and a hitter, and he's a Pittsburgh Steeler."

Taking linebackers with the opening two draft picks showed that Tomlin wanted to put his stamp on the franchise, and he made his own mark on the ensuing training camp as well when he brought the team in early and scheduled 15 grueling two-a-day practice sessions.

"I'm not approaching this as a tone-setter, looking at how this will compare to camps in the future or even how it compares to camps in the past," Tomlin said prior to the opening of his initial training camp. "Each year stands on its own, but we have to prepare to be our very best. And that's how we're going to approach it this year."

The Steelers were 10-6 during Tomlin's initial season as the head coach and won the AFC North Division. The club dropped a heart-breaking 31-29 decision to the Jacksonville Jaguars on a controversial play in a home playoff game, but that only provided an impetus for success in 2008. Tomlin determined that the Steelers needed a running back and selected Illinois product Rashard Mendenhall with their No. 1 pick. Mendenhall suffered a broken shoulder against the Baltimore Ravens during limited action as a rookie, but came back in 2009-10 to run for more than 1,000 to lead the Steelers in both years. He also led with more than 900 yards rushing in 2011, but suffered a serious knee injury in the final game and never recovered in 2012. He was not re-signed in 2013 after several character, attitude, and discipline issues marred his final seasons.

Safety Ryan Mundy from West Virginia, a Pittsburgh native, was taken in the sixth round. Like Mendenhall, Mundy remained five years with the team as a valued backup, but he was not re-signed. So, the entire 2008 draft basically was a flop for Tomlin and the staff. The remaining picks, from rounds 2-6—Texas wideout Limas Sweed, UCLA pass-rusher Bruce Davis, Texas offensive tackle Tony Hills, Oregon quarterback Dennis Dixon, and Iowa linebacker Mike Humpal—either were cut immediately or remained for a couple years without playing hardly at all. Marshall offensive lineman Doug Legursky was signed as a free agent and has been a valued backup and spot starter.

In 2009, Tomlin's first-round selection was Missouri defensive end Ziggy Hood, who entered his fifth season in

2013. He became a full-time starter in 2012 after playing extensively the year before when Aaron Smith was injured. Hood has been average thus far, but the Steelers are hopeful that he'll continue to improve during his second full season as a starter. The Steelers did not have a second-round selection, but they took Wisconsin offensive lineman Kraig Urbik and Mississippi wideout Mike Wallace in the third round. Urbik was deemed too soft to make it and eventually was cut, but he hooked on with the Buffalo Bills and has been a starter there. Wallace was among the top big-play receivers in the NFL from the minute he stepped onto the field, but after four seasons he moved on to the Miami Dolphins in free agency after an erratic 2012. Oregon State cornerback Keenan Lewis also was a third-round pick. He lasted four seasons before signing a free-agent deal with his hometown New Orleans Saints in 2013. Lewis was a valued backup early in his career, but started in 2012. He cashed in when the Steelers believed they couldn't re-sign him.

In the fifth round, the Steelers had two picks—Central Florida cornerback Joe Burnett and UNLV running back Frank Summers—and Oregon defensive lineman Sunny Harris was taken in the sixth round. Penn State center A.Q. Shipley and Arkansas State tight end David Johnson were the club's seventh-round picks. Johnson has remained with the team in a limited role, but had to come back in 2013 after being on injured reserve in 2012. Free-agent signings included offensive guard Ramon Foster from Tennessee and Bowie State running back Isaac Redman. Foster and Redman have been valued backups and starters, and both were re-signed for 2013.

The Steelers and Tomlin won the AFC North Division title for a second straight season in 2008 with a 12-4 record, as James Harrison was the defensive player of the year and the head coach received NFL coach-of-the-year honors. The Steelers beat the San Diego Chargers and Baltimore Ravens in the playoffs on their way to a stunning 27-23 win against the Arizona Cardinals in Super Bowl XLIII. Quarterback Ben Roethlisberger fired a game-winning touchdown pass to Super Bowl MVP Santonio Holmes with 35 seconds remaining. Harrison also returned an interception 100 yards for a touchdown. Gary Russell scored on a one-yard plunge, and Jeff Reed kicked two field goals. With the win, the Steelers became the first NFL franchise to capture six Super Bowls, and Tomlin became the youngest head coach to win a Lombardi Trophy.

The Steelers added to the franchise's legacy by reaching Super Bowl XLV after compiling a 12-4 record during the 2010 season. However, the Steelers could not overcome an early 18-point deficit and lost to the Green Bay Packers, 31-25, as Mendenhall fumbled to thwart a possible game-winning drive. Pro Bowl center Maurkice Pouncey didn't play due to an ankle injury, but the stage was set for success in the next decade.

Chapter 9

The 2010s

In with a Bang

While the 2009 season ended with a whimper, as the Steelers finished third in the AFC North with a 9-7 record and missed the playoffs, their average showing secured them a mid-level pick in the first round during the 2010 NFL Draft. And with the 18th overall selection, the Steelers took Florida center Maurkice Pouncey. The center position has a celebrated past with the franchise, as Ray Mansfield, Mike Webster, Dermontti Dawson, and Jeff Hartings were Pro Bowl performers and led the Steelers to the Super Bowl. Dawson was the only one who wasn't victorious in the big game, but he and Webster are enshrined in the Pro Football Hall of Fame. Justin Hartwig played in the NFL from 2002-09, including the final two seasons with the Steelers, and he was the starting center for the 2008 Super Bowl win. But he was quickly pushed out after Pouncey earned the starting job in his rookie training camp.

Pouncey has had a rousing start to his career, like his famous predecessors, with Pro Bowl selections after all three seasons (2010-12). Pouncey is strong and athletic. He can pull, if necessary, and get to the next level to take out a linebacker. Pouncey is the first center the Steelers drafted with their No. 1 pick since 1941. The last offensive lineman the Steelers took in the first round was guard Kendall Simmons in 2002.

Steelers coach Mike Tomlin beamed when he announced the Pouncey pick.

"He's a guy who we've viewed as an interior offensive lineman with position flexibility," Tomlin said. "[And] he started at right guard as a true freshman and then spent the past two years as a center. He's a young guy . . . with a great deal of experience playing high-quality ball in the SEC. He's the type of player and has the type of demeanor that we covet. He's a physical guy.

"He's football smart, and we're excited about having him. [Pouncey] has the demeanor that players have with the Steelers. He's a finisher. He's a physical football player who likes to play the game, [and] he likes everything that goes with that. He likes to work out. He likes to compete in the weight room and work at his craft. And those are things, of course, that we're looking for."

Pouncey noted that he already had an uncle who was a big Steelers fan, but the club's newest center quickly turned into one as well.

"I'm so happy to get picked by the Steelers," Pouncey said after he was drafted. "All their fans, the city, that's a team I met with at the Combine and fell in love with. So, I'm very happy right now. They weren't my favorite team growing up, but I really fell in love with them at the Combine. [And] I know they've had a lot of great centers, but I just want to continue the tradition."

Pouncey added that he had been made aware of the team's history at center.

"I know all about the guys who played center for the Steelers before me," Pouncey said. "Mike Webster, Dermontti Dawson, he called me when I got here and spoke to me when we were at training camp. There's two Hall-of-Famers right there, guys who have led this team to the Super Bowl. Jeff Hartings, those are some great players right there. I know the history, and I want to do what they did for the Steelers, help them win another Super Bowl."

In the second round, the Steelers selected Virginia Tech pass-rusher Jason Worilds. This pick had Tomlin written all over it, as the Steelers passed on Penn State linebacker Sean Lee, who went to the Dallas Cowboys three picks later. Lee became a starter in his second season at inside linebacker, a position of need for the Steelers now, while Worilds has been average as a backup due to various injuries and inconsistent play. In the third round, the Steelers got SMU wideout Emmanuel Sanders. He has been a solid possession receiver, but there is potential for Sanders to accomplish more in the future.

The Steelers had two sixth-round picks and selected Georgia Tech running back Jonathan Dwyer and Central Michigan wideout Antonio Brown. The fourth-round pick and three fifth-rounders never amounted to much. Stevenson Sylvester, an inside linebacker from Utah, played for the Steelers for three seasons. But he has been injury-prone and inconsistent. The seventh-round pick never made it, either, but Dwyer and Brown should have a bright future. Dwyer has been a solid backup running back, while Brown was a steal in the sixth round. He came on strong as a rookie and played well in the playoffs, but made a huge jump in production with more than 60 catches each in 2011 and '12. In 2011, Brown had 69 catches for 1,108 yards and also tallied more than 1,000 return yards to receive Pro Bowl honors as a punt and kickoff return man.

The Steelers won the AFC North with a 12-4 record in 2010 and got a big play from Brown to key a 31-24 divisional playoff win against the Baltimore Ravens. The Steelers stopped the New York Jets, 24-19, in the AFC championship game to qualify for the franchise's eighth Super Bowl appearance. The Steelers couldn't overcome several debilitating turnovers, however, and dropped a 31-25 decision to the Green Bay Packers. Running back Rashard Mendenhall fumbled late during a possible game-winning drive to seal the team's fate.

Incidentally, Pouncey helped the Steelers reach the playoffs, on their way to that Super Bowl, but he was unavailable for the game with an ankle injury. Safety Troy Polamalu was the NFL's defensive player of the year in 2010.

Not in the Cards

There was a lot to like about the Steelers 2011 NFL Draft, as they selected Ohio State defensive end Cameron Heyward in the first round. He's the son of Pitt legend Craig "Ironhead" Heyward with strong ties to the area. In the second round, the club returned to Florida to snag offensive tackle Marcus Gilbert. Along with center Maurkice Pouncey and left tackle Max Starks, right tackle Gilbert would give the Steelers three Gators on their offensive line.

The third and fourth rounds were used to pad the depth chart in an aging secondary, as the Steelers selected a pair of cornerbacks—Texas product Curtis Brown in the third round and The Citadel's Cortez Allen in the fourth—and after a slow start to their careers the club has hopes for a bright future for both. Allen passed Brown on the depth chart, however, and is expected to be a starting cornerback for years to come for the Steelers.

The remaining picks—linebacker Chris Carter in the fifth round, offensive lineman Keith Williams in the sixth, and running back Baron Batch in the seventh—have not made an impact. Williams was cut, and Batch has been injured, for the most part. And when he played, he didn't do much. Carter started three games for the Steelers in 2012, but he played just eight games as a rookie in 2011 and eight the next season due to injuries and largely was ineffective.

The Steelers finished an amazing 12-4 for the second straight season, but placed second in the AFC North to the Baltimore Ravens, who also were 12-4. The Steelers won a key game in Baltimore the previous season to earn the division title, but were destroyed at Baltimore in the season-opener in 2011 and lost 23-20 at home after the defense made quarterback Joe Flacco look like Joe Montana during a game-winning, 13-play, 92-yard touchdown drive in 2:16. Flacco hit wideout Torrey Smith with a 26-yard scoring pass with just eight seconds left to bury the Steelers.

The club rebounded from a rough 2-2 start, but quarterback Ben Roethlisberger hurt his foot in a loss at Houston, and he struggled the rest of the season with a couple different injuries. Safety Troy Polamalu also was banged up during the season, but never missed a game, although he rarely practiced at the end and wasn't as active. Roethlisberger missed just one game, but he should have sat out a late-season loss at San Francisco to rest for the regular-season homestretch and the post-season. The quarterback played because the Steelers still could have won the division with a win against the 49ers. Instead, the club limped into a wild-card playoff game at Denver and lost a heartbreaker, 29-23, as quarterback Tim Tebow connected with wideout Demaryius Thomas for an 80-yard touchdown reception on the first play in overtime.

After all the ups and downs during the 2011 season, it seemed to be fitting for the Steelers to get "Tebowed" in Denver to force a shakeup in the near future.

The Page Turns

Following the 2011 season, the Steelers released long-time veterans, and fan favorites, Hines Ward, Aaron Smith, James Farrior and Chris Hoke. And each announced his retirement before the 2012 season. The Steelers clearly moved on, but not up in the standings. Actually, they dropped to third place behind the playoff-bound Baltimore Ravens and Cincinnati Bengals with an 8-8 record and remained home for the postseason for the second time in Tomlin's tenure.

The youth movement continued on the offensive line, as Stanford guard David DeCastro was taken by the Steelers in the first round during the 2012 NFL Draft. The rebuilt offensive line continued to take shape, as they chose Ohio State tackle Mike Adams in the second round. By all accounts, DeCastro and Adams should be starters for a long time in the NFL. The same fate was expected for third-round selection Sean Spence, an inside linebacker from Miami, Florida, but a serious knee injury during the preseason—where several ligaments were damaged—forced him to miss the entire 2012 season and could threaten his career advancement as well.

The Steelers hoped they snagged Casey Hampton's replacement in the fourth round with Washington nose tackle Alameda Ta'amu. However, these plans were derailed after Ta'amu was charged and later convicted of reckless endangerment, resisting arrest, and drunken driving. Another factor that contributed to Ta'amu's spending the 2012 season on the bench was strong play from young backup Steve McLendon. Ta'amu's playing status could change in the future, however, but he would have to earn his spot with off- and on-field improvements. In the fifth round, the Steelers chose speedy Florida running back Chris Rainey. But after a season with more than 1,000 total yards, including a promising start as a kickoff return man, domestic abuse charges shortly after the season forced the club to release Rainey.

The Steelers had four seventh-round picks—wideout Toney Clemons, who played football scholastically in the Pittsburgh area, tight end David Paulson, cornerback Terrence Frederick, and offensive lineman Kelvin Beachum. Clemons was on the practice squad much of 2012, but eventually was claimed by Jacksonville Jaguars and played four games for them. Paulson eventually became the Steelers No. 2 tight end behind Heath Miller. Frederick never made it to the season, while Beachum played in seven games with five straight starts at right tackle to close the season. Beachum was drafted as a guard and could play there in the future with the Steelers. By the end of the 2012 season, the Steelers were playing two rookies, DeCastro and Beachum, on the right side of their offensive line. And it's somewhat ironic that the player who was nearly Mr. Irrelevant, eventually became Mr. Indispensable for the Steelers.

Beachum was the 248th overall selection in 2012, and only five players were chosen after him. The final pick, which is termed Mr. Irrelevant, was 253rd overall during the 2012 NFL Draft.

"I had no idea who was going to draft me until the Steelers called, so I was just waiting for that call to come," Beachum said. "There had been a couple teams who called me and talked about maybe signing me after the draft [as a free agent]. I really don't remember who those teams were, but I was confident that I'd get drafted. And fortunately, I got drafted by a good team."

After injuries to the Steelers' two most recent second-round picks, Marcus Gilbert and Adams, Beachum was pressed into a starting role at right offensive tackle. Gilbert started five games at right tackle before an ankle injury that never healed correctly placed him on injured reserve, while Adams—Gilbert's replacement—started six games before being shelved by a severe ankle injury. Beachum's first NFL start came on the road against the Baltimore Ravens, and he had a strong finish in the regular season.

"I got a ton of advice from our veterans," Beachum said. "Some guys had their first starts against the Ravens [Willie Colon and Ramon Foster], and they've had some success against them. So, they had some good input going into the game. And as we all saw, things worked out pretty well for us down there."

A Texas native, Beachum played collegiately at SMU. The Mustangs offered him a scholarship, along with Iowa State and Division I-AA schools Stephen F. Austin and West Texas A&M. And after nearly going undrafted, the Steelers decided to take a chance late in the seventh round. That wasn't the case for DeCastro, who chose the Cardinals out of high school over a myriad of suitors. He was a consensus first-round pick, but the Steelers believed they were fortunate to get him late in the opening round with the 24th overall selection and targeted him to be the starting right guard from the outset. But the turf at Buffalo had something else in mind. DeCastro suffered a serious knee injury in the third preseason game there and was not activated until Nov. 26. He played on special teams—the field-goal unit—December 9, 2012, during a home game with San Diego, and then DeCastro started the final three regular-season games.

"I think both those guys, David and Kelvin, we expect a lot from them," veteran left tackle Max Starks said. "Kelvin had a great Baltimore game, and we all had a rough San Diego game. But Kelvin is a kid who's very strong mentally, so it didn't affect him. David, he was a first-round pick, and he has a lot of talent. I think he was on the rise until he got hurt in the preseason at Buffalo. But he worked very hard in practice. I think we have a good tandem on our right side."

DeCastro and Beachum had just one full week of practice together.

"He's obviously a smart guy, and I think we've worked well together," DeCastro said. "It was great to see a guy like Kelvin step into the right tackle spot on this O-line and have some success after just a couple games. It was great to see a rookie do that, and seeing how well he fit in certainly gives me more confidence as well. I waited a long time (to start), but that's life. Adversity comes along, but how well you deal with it is the key to success. And I think I've dealt with it pretty well so far."

Beachum came a long way during his rookie season.

"You learn pretty quick that in the NFL, you need to be ready to play every week," Beachum said. "You can't take any player or any team for granted, and that's the way I look at it. The guys across from me get paid like I get paid, although they might get paid a little more than me, but you get the idea.

"The difference for me was the intensity. I knew it would be intense, but every single play is a battle. People are playing for their livelihoods, their families and their health, so they want to get the best of me every time. So, you need to go out there and put your best foot forward on every snap or you'll get beat."

After the 2012 season ended, Ramon Foster referenced former first-round picks Pouncey at center and DeCastro at right guard and second-round selections Gilbert and Adams at tackle as key components to future Steelers offensive lines.

"I think the average age in our room now is 25 years old," Foster said. "Those guys are really good. I think everyone in our room now has played. We have depth. We just have to get everybody healthy this offseason and see how everything transpires.

"[So], I think we have a lot of talented and special players on the line. You have all dynamics, smart guys and tough guys, every type of dynamic in the room. The talent is bottomless right now. I want to be a part of a line like that. Barring injuries, it could be a really special line."

Foster's future with the Steelers was up in the air, but the team re-signed him once free agency began after the 2012 season. The near future of the franchise is a bit up in the air as well, as veterans like James Harrison and Max Starks were not re-signed early in the offseason. Also, former starters Mike Wallace, Rashard Mendenhall, and Keenan Lewis signed free-agent contracts with other teams.

So, as they have done many times before, the Steelers must turn the page to a new chapter in franchise history.